WHY DOES GOD HATE ME?

Stephanie Harrington
Published by CREATE HER
3408 South Atlantic Avenue
PMB #53
Daytona Beach Shores, Florida 32118

First CREATE HER Publishing, November 2024

Why Does God Hate Me?
The Reach Beyond Human Comprehension
Copyright © Stephanie Harrington, 2024

ISBN
979-8-9913054-0-2 Paperback
979-8-9913054-1-9 EPUB

Cover Designed by SheerGenius
Editorial & Book Compilation Services
by Pen to Press by Ladero

Scripture quotations marked KJV are King James Version.
The KJV is public domain in the United States of America.

STEPHANIE HARRINGTON

WHY DOES GOD HATE ME?

THE REACH BEYOND HUMAN COMPREHENSION

CREATE HER
EVOLVING TO EXIST

TABLE OF CONTENTS

INTRODUCTION

Life is filled with moments that leave us questioning everything we thought we knew. "Why does God hate me?" It is a question born from pain, frustration, and the feeling of abandonment. This book is not about condemning the question but exploring the depth of that pain and finding a way to grow through it instead of getting through it.

In my first book, *Evolve: Activate the Gift Within*, I explored the power of self-discovery and stepping into our true potential. This journey laid the foundation for understanding that the answers we seek are often within us.

Why Does God Hate Me? picks up where *Evolve* left off and invites you to look inward and confront the uncomfortable truth that the source of your struggles may be the stories you tell yourself.

It is about unmasking the mystery of the self, accepting the hard truths, and realizing that the power to change your reality lies within you.

The victim mentality has become a growing concern in today's society, with more people feeling disempowered or perceiving themselves as passive recipients of their circumstances. Research shows that the rise in feelings of victimization is linked to various factors, including cultural, psychological, and social influences. Studies suggest that up to 70% of people have at some point engaged in some form of victim mentality or behavior, where they feel helpless or blame external forces for their struggles.

But here's the truth: sometimes, we have to get it wrong to get it right. It is through our missteps, our moments of feeling lost or stuck, that we learn the most. The path out of the victim mentality begins when we realize we are not powerless.

The challenge is recognizing this unconscious behavior and learning to shift from a victim mindset to a position of self-empowerment. By breaking free from the victim mentality and beginning to create healthier, more authentic realities, individuals can regain control over their lives.

This book invites you to embrace that process, to recognize that mistakes are part of the path to self-awareness and that every wrong turn is an opportunity to find your way forward. The power to evolve, heal, and rewrite your story is within you. In these pages, you will find the tools to break free from that illusion and begin unmasking your true self.

CHAPTER ONE:
THE BANDIT DILEMMA

"Hello, Susan. Can I call you back in a little while? I am on a field trip at a Nuclear Pharmacy with my classmates right now."

"It's bad," she said, and I could tell it was by the tone of her voice.

Feeling the gravity of the situation, I did not want the attention of further embarrassment. I turned aside and walked away to get some privacy.

"What happened?" I whispered with nervous concern.

"Well, you're not gonna believe what he did." She paused.

Then, in a faint rumbling of her voice, she said, "He robbed a bank, and the FBI is looking for him."

Speechless could not describe my reaction to the news of my husband's action. I hung up the phone and asked my classmate (with whom I carpooled) if we could leave immediately. I told her I had an emergency. Without hesitation or question, she said, "Let's go!" and off we went.

On our way back, my classmate kept talking to me on the car ride without knowing what had happened; however, I was not listening to anything she was saying. It was like I was not in the car or my body. My mind was racing with all the different scenarios of what had happened. What my mother-in-law just shared with me seemed unreal. I thought to myself, *Is this some joke?* The closer I got to the house, the more anxious I felt. By the time we exited the highway, the palms of my hands were sweaty, and my heart was beating fast, pounding on my ribcage. I did not want my classmate to know what was happening, so I tried to look normal, even though I felt a faint flush on my cheeks, and my forehead was cold.

The car stopped, and we said our goodbyes. I exited, jumped into my car, and headed home. I parked my car, took a deep breath, tried to gather my thoughts, exited the car, and walked to my front door. My head sounded like a marching band; all I could hear was my heartbeat banging through my temples and into my eardrums. The vibration of my pulse throughout my entire body was throbbing. My thoughts flip-flopped between believing and not believing my husband had robbed a bank. Feeling this mind-blowing devastation, I approached the door to face our nineteen-month-old daughter. I dreaded my daughter looking back at me as I experienced the feelings of loss, shame, and fear. I was trembling, knowing I could do nothing to fix this. I grabbed my baby from my mother-in-law's hands and held her tightly. Then I cried out hysterically and asked myself, "WHY ME?"

My daughter had no idea what was happening. Her innocence was ripped through my perception. Holding her in my arms, I felt as if I were holding on for dear life. From the corner of my eye, I glimpsed guns and more guns, and men clad in armor outside the window. Then, the door burst open, and they came running through my house, calling out my husband's name. "Come out! Come out now!" they shouted.

I stood in one spot and squeezed my baby in my arms to cover her like a shield as everything in me froze. I sensed silence, and at the same time, it seemed very loud. It was like everything was moving in slow motion.

"He is not here!" I shouted. "He is not here!"

But no one seemed to pay attention to what I was saying. It was such an uncomfortable situation.

They marched through the house while shouting his name, "Come out! Come out!"

They kept yelling, but he was not there. Forced to stand tall, embracing the severity of the situation, I stood with my back against the wall, anticipating the next move. Uncomfortable, unsettled, and mentally dissociated, I convinced myself to keep breathing. My panic was not more substantial than our baby girl in my hands.

But what do you do when a hammer hits you on the head, and you never see it coming? *Am I alive? Could this be a dream? And if it is, can someone wake me up, please?* At times, we had moments of shaking and rattling of the cradle, but robbing a bank rocked our family's cradle to pieces that June morning. The uneasiness and uncertainty of whether or not it was the end or beginning of our family dominated my attention.

Dear reader, get ready to take a trip down memory lane with me to explore a mindset and belief system that will undoubtedly evoke unimaginable emotions in you. Let me take you back in time to the morning of the bank robbery, mainly through my perception and my reality at that moment in time.

It was about 6 a.m. when I dropped my daughter off with my husband that morning. He was staying at my mother-in-law's house because we were separated. I was already running late, and I was carpooling with one of my classmates. I was to meet her at a particular spot and did not want to be late. I turned my left turn indicator on as I was about to turn into the driveway and pulled into a closer parking spot near my mother-in-law's apartment. I parked the car, unbuckled my seat belt, and exited the vehicle.

Just for a moment, I gazed down the walkway where my husband would walk to meet me and saw a shadow walking towards me. I said, "Good, I will be on time."

I opened the back seat, took our baby out of the car seat, grabbed her bags, and quickly walked to meet her dad. He seemed like he was patiently waiting to see us.

"Good morning," I said to him and quickly turned my attention to our little girl.

I spoke softly, "Be a good little girl for daddy today, ok, my munchkin."

He took our daughter from me, smiled, and tried to kiss me, but because we were not in good standing, I gave him the cold shoulder and a look that just was not pleasant. He tried to converse with me, but I insisted; I had to leave because I did not want my classmate waiting for me. But my action was intended as vengeance for my grief over our relationship status.

It is amusing how our feelings and actions towards someone can change quickly after the honeymoon stage in a relationship. The once blissful butterflies in my stomach now seemed elusive. How did we get here? How long are we going to stay here? Is this part of the grand plan for my life? I did not have the answers to these questions, nor did my husband.

As I walked away and opened the car door to get in and take off, softly spoken but with much intensity and deliberateness, my husband said, "No matter what, just remember that I love you."

When he said that to me, I looked at him but did not answer; I responded, *Yeah, yeah, blah blah* in my mind. I gave him that kind of look—the one that says, "Just shut up already."

I closed the car door and immediately drove off. While driving down the street, I reminisced about what he said to me and thought his tone seemed slightly different from any other. *I love you.* I replayed it over in my head, questioning his motive, but then did not think anything of it.

Finally, I met up with my classmate. We had a long drive ahead of us. During the drive, I shifted my focus to my thoughts. Spending time in my head is considered normal for me. Whenever I am perplexed about anything, I internalize it and try to sort things out. It doesn't matter who is around me; I just get lost going over all the scenarios and possible what-ifs. It depends on what I am facing at that particular moment. The pressing issue at that moment was the separation between my husband and me. Reflecting on past events can sometimes bring regret or a desire for different outcomes, but I never considered challenging myself to wonder if what I wanted was not what I needed.

My home life was like a battlefield. It felt like a war zone with the constant bombing of grenades and machine guns shooting bullets in every direction. There was never a scarcity of artillery weapons. Every day, it seemed like a new shipment would arrive as a toxic but burning issue. I chose my weapon of choice, and he would choose his weapon of choice. Not only were we always with our weapons loaded and ready for any attack, we were also trying to protect the war zone from any outside threat. Our uniforms were fatigued with camouflage patterns to help distract the critics but good enough to blend in with the surroundings. We both loved our families, and wanted them to stay connected to our base—our home. We would try our best to protect them, thinking the attack was from external sources. We were so caught up in the war that we never stopped for a moment and considered that we might be the source of our affliction. Instead, we spent much time strategizing, worrying, and fighting for peace, hoping that someone or something would give it to us instead of searching within ourselves.

Every day, it seemed like the war only worsened; we were never closer to agreeing and understanding each other. Before I met my husband, I was a general in the jungle, and I fought all my battles with one weapon: fear. I knew how to plan tactics to combat any attack that looked or felt like a threat. I even knew how to hide very well. I fought all my battles by myself, starting from an early age. I taught myself to be a self-sufficient survivor. There was no need to join forces with another general even though we were on the same side. Letting go of control was a far-fetched idea for me, even without the awareness that was my mindset. I was from the jungle, and he was from the streets. After all, he knew nothing about the lions, tigers, and bears that appeared in my life as my past sufferings. My angle was this: he needed to follow my lead and learn to care for and watch over us. And I was to show him how I fought my misfortune. I am not saying I did an excellent job caring for myself, but it was enough to keep me alive in the jungle.

I did not realize then that I was carrying what I now call the silent killer of overthinking. I used the term "silent killer" because thinking is considered an everyday norm; you should think about everything, especially if it is a life-altering decision. But how do you measure your thoughts? How do you know when to stop thinking? How do you know what the limit is? Am I doing too much or too little? Am I hurting myself or helping myself? I had no awareness of these questions and needed clarity and much understanding.

Overthinking coupled with fear is a sign that says "OFF LIMITS!" "Do not enter this war zone." That, however, was not my reality. Analytical thinking was my norm. I would spend most of my day contemplating what had happened in my past and simultaneously worrying about my future.

Overthinking became a daily ritual, which, in turn, shaped my mindset, perceptions, and beliefs. I trained daily, working out my mind muscle through overthinking push-ups, fear jumping jacks, trying to quench the thirst for worry and anxiety, readying myself for war, and preparing myself to counter any attack.

But who was attacking me? Was it my thoughts? Did I even know I was overthinking everything? What were the symptoms of overthinking? I needed to ask myself these questions, but how do you seek an answer when you do not even know there is a problem? I would entertain every thought that popped up in my mind. The health of my mind was not a priority. I did not know how to filter through thoughts and care for my mental health. Instead, I would allow my mind to be occupied with thoughts in a continuous cycle daily, feeding my mind with the same thoughts - growing and expanding my damnation. I was giving it all my attention and energy.

Going through a separation from my husband was just another mental battle I was not prepared for, but my life experience taught me how to dig tunnels, climb walls, and keep moving, even when wounded. Every wound and every scar bolstered my willpower and strengthened my courage and determination. Therefore, whenever I faced any strenuous situation, I would reassure myself that I was strong and could get through it. It never dawned on me that it would be better to *grow through* the situation rather than get through it.

Motivated by a fear of failure, I relentlessly delved into treacherous tunnels and navigated perilous minefields, all in pursuit of the prestigious Legion of Merit Medal. Although this medal symbolizes exceptional service and accomplishments, my underlying motive was a craving for attention. Countless hours were spent meticulously analyzing the war zone, repeatedly replaying each attack in my mind. As these scenes unfolded, they triggered unsettling emotions, often centered around mundane incidents such as my husband's failure to answer a phone call.

In these moments of reflection, I would construct elaborate explanations for his behavior, embracing these self-generated assumptions as undeniable truths. I would allow these internal narratives to shape my perception of reality despite lacking a factual basis. The resulting emotions became the evidence I clung to, a means to demonstrate to my superiors the emotional toll this war exacted upon us. Regrettably, I would convince myself of these falsehoods and unjustly expect my husband to take responsibility for the products of my imagination.

Caught between a desire to fight for our relationship and the harsh reality of us becoming adversaries, I often pondered whether we were truly united in our cause or merely embroiled in a battle against each other. The conflicting emotions within me yearned for both fear and respect from my husband, creating a complex dynamic that blurred our boundaries. I fought hard, treading the line between fighting for us and fighting each other.

Why do I ponder our motives? Fear was a tactic that was used on me, and it kept me scared and respectful, so I thought, why not use it on him? It will give me what I want and keep the peace; I meant well. I never aimed to hurt anyone; I sought a safe place to call home. I wanted what I thought I never had. My decorated self-image was fighting for an existence. I had never cared for any other uniform, and I knew all too well about other self-image dress codes. I focused all my attention on the one I wore and made it more presentable whenever I faced the public.

It did not take long for my tough exterior to crack open, and I was not ready to address the broken-spirited child waiting to be heard and felt. *Ignore yourself and focus all your attention on the General!* That was my approach. Watch every move he makes, and do not let him out of your sight. Nothing the General did was ever good enough for me. I was always tough on him; my expectations came with a price. My unidentified attitude was that he should prove he could care for our family and earn my trust.

Conversely, my husband, the General, needed to figure out what I wanted. He was just giving me what he thought I needed. And at the same time, he was looking for what he felt he needed from me. We were both playing the offense-defense game.

Two wounded soldiers on one glorified battleground, our strength and bravery drove our strategic opinionated fighting skills. But was this necessary for the invisible war of shame, fear, and indifference? Could robbing a bank be the end of another battle? Or was it the beginning of another journey? The suspense was too much for me, and the situation was too grand for my speculation. I have wandered away most of my life, overthinking and overcompensating to get what I wanted. It became a tease, a roller coaster ride with no laughter or screaming of us having fun. Did he give up on us, I question? Did he quit the squad and leave us hanging in the danger zone? What will be next? What other adventure awaits us?

Asking questions to which you do not want answers is hard to swallow. Have you ever been in a situation where you feel like time has stopped, and everything you are experiencing seems like a dream? A dream that knows you very well, but you know nothing about it. All eyes are on me, even my own. The center of attention shifts from watching the General to the world watching me.

What are you going to do now, courageous woman? Everyone is waiting. You have a reputation to uphold; show no signs of weakness. You made promises to yourself. Are you going to let this situation threaten your commitments?

Deep inside, part of me says I no longer want to be strong. If I am honest, I am afraid and have no jurisdiction or influence. This act is massive. This is the first time I have seen something like it. My hands are tied, my mind is blank, and my mouth is speechless.

I reach for my rifle, but no ammunition is firing, only silence hitting the wall and empty shells dropping to the ground. Am I now another single mother on the frontline? This was my past, not our daughter's future. Did we repeat the same cycle? Did we pass down the chains of suffering to our daughter? Did we fight a good fight for her? Did we fight for her, or did we fight for ourselves? If not so, what were we fighting? Was it a feeling, emotion, perception, belief, or something I (or we) did in the name of love?

CHAPTER TWO:
THE UNEXPECTED CALL

When I received the phone call, it was one of those moments. These moments may sometimes be called the crossroads in our lives, the midnight hour, or when our backs are against the wall. For some, it may be their breaking point or a wake-up call. For others, it may be growth and expansion or higher awareness. It could be the moment you wish to ignore or hope would never come due to fear of the unknown.

As I sat in the living room with my baby in my arms, a mix of suspense and mental panic coursed through me. When I heard my husband's name being called out and witnessed the door swinging open, my heart beat a little faster. The sight before me was a sea of guns, more guns, and voices relentlessly echoing his name.

"He is not here!" I shouted, desperately hoping they would hear and believe me, prompting a pause for conversation. They were, however, on their mission.

"He is not here! He is not here!" I repeated.

It felt like I was invisible, but I understood why I was ignored. They were inside a stranger's home and did not know what to expect. An air of uncertainty hung in the room as myriad thoughts swirled within me.

While the officers walked through our home, the noise and chatter created a disorienting atmosphere of a nightmarish ordeal. I was seated with my baby tightly in my arms with tears streaming down my face, but I had yet to fully comprehend the full extent of the situation. My heart pounded relentlessly in my chest, amplifying the moment's intensity. My hands trembled, sweaty, and I unconsciously tapped my right foot in an irregular rhythm. Every fiber of my being yearned for time to freeze, but unfortunately, this unsettling reality was my reality.

A growing number of authorities encircled the perimeter of our house. I had never witnessed such overwhelming attention in such proximity. How could I have seen such a thing? As I stated before, I was a small-town country girl who was not exposed to real-life drama. The atmosphere became stifling, like a scorching bath on a hot summer day; I only wished for an escape as the intensity seared my skin. Though daylight persisted, darkness reigned like a shadow within the room.

Not knowing what would transpire next, I stayed seated and waited for the ringing in my ears to stop. Or the boots on the ground to slow down. Lights were flashing, and the sirens were getting louder and louder. It looked like Christmas at our home, with different colors, lights flashing, and people walking in and out of my house. And all I could do was sit there and wait, not knowing what I was waiting for. I knew who they were and what they represented, but they did not know who I was and what I represented. The feeling of unease was like standing at borders no one wants to cross, but I knew I must.

You never know what you can endure until you have endured it.

Finally, all the rooms were searched, and my husband was nowhere to be found.

The sky looked blue, and the sun was raging hot outside, a perfect day for the beach. The beach, however, was the last thing on my mind. I would have traded that day for a beach day if it were up to me. While all the commotion was happening, I tried to distract myself by focusing on our baby in my hands. Her ignorance of the situation at hand provided me with a bit of ease regarding the potential of any lasting trauma from this nightmare we were both having to endure.

I find immense joy in being an early riser, relishing the precious moments of solitude before the world awakens. As soon as my alarm sounds, I am propelled into action without a second thought. Dressing and preparing for the day come effortlessly, as my routines have become ingrained like a well-rehearsed dance.

That day marked a significant milestone as our class embarked on our long-awaited field trip to a Nuclear Pharmacy. At that time, I was a student at Barry University and an intern at Jackson Memorial Hospital's Nuclear Medicine Technologist Program. I was looking forward to venturing beyond the confines of the clinical setting and stepping outside the classroom or hospital floor.

My current situation, however, had me residing with my father, which added to my morning routine since my dad's house was further away from my mother-in-law's home, where I had to drop off our baby. I factored in approximately twenty minutes for the commute, allowing ample time for a smooth transition. Before anything else, I loaded the necessary bags, car seats, and stroller into the car, prioritizing their placement for convenience. Once everything was in order, I secured my baby in the car seat, and off we went.

As the engine purred, I turned on music, selecting uplifting melodies that inspired my spirit. I loved to listen to music while I drive. The words of encouragement served as a wellspring of inner strength, providing a refreshing energy boost. I do not doubt that my baby girl loved to listen to music while riding in the car. After dropping the baby off in my husband's care, I took off for the designated meeting point.

Finally, I reached the spot where my classmate and I had decided to meet. I felt good knowing we were both on time. We had planned the carpooling arrangements to ride together and share in the collective excitement and anticipation. As we merged onto the road, our conversations filled the air, setting the tone for the day.

We quickly huddled with our program director and headed inside the building. The preparation and handling of radioactive material piqued our curiosity. We were adequately dressed for the occasion. We had lab coats, handbooks, notepads, radioactive sensor badges, and many questions. Finally, it was time for our first break and time to get some fresh air. As we were walking out of the building, I got THE CALL!

At times, moments of opportunity or self-fulfilling prophecies present themselves just as you are about to take a break or call it quits.

What do you think about when your whole life is like a movie? From my experience, YOU THINK ABOUT NOTHING. That day, time felt like it stopped, and everything slowed down. I believe it is because I was being present. I was not thinking about the day before or the next, and my mind was not wandering. Being present gave me a bitter taste as if my life were a lie; there was no music playing in the background or grand opening of the curtains. My mouth was dry, I felt parched, and the uncomfortable, raw experience left me with no taste in my mouth.

The functions of my internal organs were still running, like a standard operation, even though my mind was over-occupied. Thank goodness our bodies do not stop functioning when problems arise. *Who should I call?* I asked myself. *Should I call my husband?* I wondered, but what if he did not answer? What if he were dead? Or, what if he *does* answer? What would I say? The unknown, curiosity, concern, and fright propel my thoughts to question an unknown answer. Dear reader, I suspect you may think, *"You haven't called him yet?!"*

It is a different feeling when you are in the situation. I did not want to face what was on the other side of the phone call. I wanted to know, but at the same time, I did *not* want to know. The conflict of interest held my mind hostage in creating my scenarios.

Finally, one of the officers told me to get some water and have a seat. I got up, entered the kitchen, and poured myself a glass of water. They, too, had some water, and it seemed like we were getting ready to settle down. I drank my water, put the glass in the sink, stood there momentarily, took a deep breath, and walked back over to the chair.

"State your name for our records, please," he said.

"Stephanie Harrington," I replied.

He asked, "Do you know why we are here?"

I burst out crying. I could not hold it together. All I could think was Please, this is not real. Make it go away. *The devastation and heartbrokenness were more painful than I had ever felt. I put my hands over my mouth and shook my head up and down, signifying, "Yes, yes, I know why you are here."*

They showed me a picture of my husband leaning over the counter at the bank. They asked me to identify him.

I stared at the picture in disbelief and asked the officers, "Do you know where he is?"

He paused and said nothing, but his gesture was more of, "I can't give any definite information now."

Have you ever been in a situation where you felt like you would do anything to bargain with God? Yep, that's precisely where I was. "Please, God, make this go away," "I am begging you," "Keep him alive," "I will do anything." "Please let this situation go away." These were my pleas.

I have been through some dark moments in my life, but nothing ever this big before. Watching stories about a bank robbery on the news is like a "shaking my head" moment; make your judgment and walk away with no attachment. But this time, it was my husband's story being told on the news, and I was not walking away from the screen, and it was hard to accept that this was even real. We are just regular people living everyday lives. How could this happen?

While bargaining with God, the officer still sought information about my husband. He asked, "Is this the shirt he left the house in this morning?"

"Well, I was not home, sir. I was on a field trip with my school when I got a call from my mother-in-law."

The cop replied, "But is this his shirt? Do you recognize it?" I took the picture from him and looked at it again, but honestly, I was not looking at the shirt; I was looking at the man in the window at the counter.

What are you thinking? I thought. Have you gone mad? How could you allow this to happen to us? While holding the picture with my eyes looking down, captivating the image but thinking about the moment. The officer leaned forward to tap the pen on his finger, using his eyes to communicate.

"I am still waiting for your reply, madam."

I slowly rolled my eyes upward, lifted my head, stared the officer in his eyes, and said, "Yes, sir, that is his shirt."

He quickly wrote down something on his paper and hesitated to ask the following question, but then he got up and walked away looking puzzled or sensitive to the situation. During this time of questioning, my baby fell asleep in my arms, so I asked if I could go and lay her down on the bed. And they said yes. I went into the room where no one was. I laid her down and kissed her on the forehead. The house got a bit muggy because the doors were left open due to the traffic in and out. My baby was sweating more than usual on the hot summer day. I wiped her sweat and cracked open a window above her to let some fresh air in. I stood there momentarily and thought, Will he see you grow up? Are you even going to know who your father is? All I could think of was, "I am so sorry, my baby girl." I wished I could make it stop. I wished I could change things; I hoped this was a dream.

I was looking down at our daughter and facing the reality that my greatest fear had become my reality. And everything I was running from showed up at my doorstep. I never thought in a million years that my belief about what I do not want could still show up, even without being an active player. Could it be the energy and attention I give it? Could it be me, keeping it alive and strengthening its existence daily? But I did not do anything wrong. It was not I who robbed the bank. You would think that what you do not want, you will not get. And what you do want, you get.

This seems logical. Not only does it seem logical, but it sounds good, too. That was my train of thought. All the training in the jungle could not prepare me enough for my current battle.

I fought hard for a family of my own. I wanted what I believed I did not have growing up. Looking at my daughter from the corner of my eyes, she slept so gently. I affirmed to myself that I had lost the battle. I let her down, I let the little girl inside me down, and I let my hopes down. I did not keep the agreement I created out of pain. Yes, I did not physically rob the bank, and no, it is not my fault my husband committed such a crime. It was not my exact words when I mentioned fearing not having a family to call my own. Instead, it was my deep-rooted belief. Daily, I was fueled by the belief that everything would go wrong. As a little girl, I experienced feelings of abandonment, rejection, and hopelessness due to sexual abuse and emotional trauma.

My attention and focus always sought security, comfort, and belonging, running from my worst nightmare. My mind was programmed to carry out the mission of finding sanctuary by trying to escape anything that seemed like a threat. Now, even if security were looking me dead in the face, I would not have recognized it because I did not know what it felt like in the first place. I only knew what it looked like based on what was displayed around me.

What I envisioned for myself was an image of what society portrayed it should look like. But not what it should *feel* like. The feelings I associated with wanting a family were fear of losing what I had or not fully accepting that what I had was accurate. I consistently feared it would be taken away, and I carried the feeling of being on the run as a child while living as an adult. I was robbing myself of my mental and emotional freedom by contradicting the free flow of "As Is" with what-ifs.

What if something goes wrong? What if I am not a good enough wife? What if he stops loving me? What if I stop arguing so much? What if he thinks I am not caring enough? What if I compromise a little? What if I try to prove how loyal I am? What if I make him feel special? What if he feels trapped? What if I do more household chores? What if I become more spiritual?

What if the pathway was inevitable? It was never so precise with each statement written above but mainly presented itself as a feeling, a feeling you wanted to escape from at all costs. The little girl inside did not speak; she felt. She lived through her imagination, she wondered. She waited, she watched, and she tried to analyze and predict.

She was waiting for her freedom to live freely, wholeheartedly, and boldly. She did not feel she could give it to herself. She believed her husband could give it to her, but to her surprise, her husband's assurance could not give it to her either. Therefore, she continued to assume the role of victim, digging herself deeper and deeper into the shadows, waging an unconscious war with herself.

She felt trapped in the minefield, with grenades going off, and daily, her dream of getting killed by one; she was losing the battle but still believed in winning the war. The expectation was her main deceiver of herself and those around her. She expected proof from her husband. She expected proof from her friends and family. She expected proof from the world. Proof she would not be hurt. Proof they could be trusted. Proof she was not being used. Proof her life mattered. Regardless of their roles in her life, she placed a high demand on people that had yet to figure it out.

But what did she have in her possession at all times? A weapon, perhaps, or a key, and if so, what kind of weapon or key? The weapon or key is Belief. Belief can mislead or blind you. Belief can make or break you. Belief is the foundation for building anything--business, building, or plans.

CHAPTER THREE:
WHO PULLS THE TRIGGER

"Belief Can Build & Kill"

My belief in fear kept me a prisoner in my mind for many years. Belief is a powerful tool for creating something wonderful, but it can also be destructive. A belief ignites willpower and pursues its cause. Belief is a focus mechanism that carries out a mission or intention meaningfully. All that is required to create a belief is the acceptance that something exists or is true. Belief has two sides: one side is for, and another is against, until proven otherwise.

Beliefs become conscious the moment they are created and accepted, and they fight for their existence to remain alive in your mind. When you hear or learn something, your acceptance plays a role in processing that information. The more convincing the conviction, the stronger the trust, and the deeper and firmer the foundation or root is planted. Whether we like it or not, our belief is a very influential force. It governs our lives in more ways than you can imagine. Our belief shapes the way we interact, communicate, and connect. Our belief shapes our identity and how we make decisions.

Have you ever stopped and asked yourself how your beliefs are formed? If not, you are not alone. I, too, never questioned the creation of my beliefs. I had no interest in my self-awareness, mental limitations, intelligence, and much more, which played a significant role in why I did not challenge my beliefs. Beliefs about myself, wealth, poverty, race, social status, politics, the economy, personal and social relationships, religion, and overall world perception.

Contemporary psychologists state that a child's behavioral patterns, beliefs, and habits are deeply embedded in their subconscious by age seven. These early formations are influenced by family, friends, financial situation, environment, culture, and traditions. As I journeyed into my past, I sought to unravel the makeup that influenced my early developmental environment. I realized that my childhood confidence was far more potent and accepting than an adult's. Then, I had to ask myself, *What potent belief still operates within me?*

With much self-reflection and research, my answer took me back to the little girl waiting to be unleashed. Waiting to be validated, waiting to be comforted, waiting for apologies and acknowledgment, waiting for vindication, waiting to hear, "Well done. You did your best" -- *waiting to live.* In Jamaica, we have a saying, "One day, one day you will see" or "Meh sah mi can't wait" (in Jamaican patois voice).

As we mature, our beliefs become more susceptible to scrutiny, leaving room for doubt and uncertainty. With age comes increased exposure to diverse perspectives and experiences, which can challenge and test the solidity of our existing beliefs. The need for validation and the desire to express our ideas become crucial in maintaining confidence in our evolving beliefs. For instance, consider the following scenario:

A diverse background group discusses growing up through the lens of cultural conditioning. Each expresses their opinions or beliefs based on their life experience, limitations, and exposure. Remember that not everyone in the discussion has an open mindset and learns how to respect others' perceptions. Still, everyone's perspective or belief is at the top of their mind. It is at the top of their mind because their belief is defending its existence. The course of action each chooses to narrate their story depends entirely on their understanding. For instance, someone is sharing a story that evokes shame in themselves. That person's driving force behind a belief influences their decision-making. It may also be expressed through actions like holding their head down, not looking into the eyes of another, or quickly steering away from the subject.

As an idea takes root and consistently manifests in your thoughts and actions, it gains acceptance and confidence. It becomes ingrained in your mind, assuming its personality and identity. This is often when people say, "I am just that way," as the habit becomes a part of their daily expression.

This expression will only change once the person develops a growth mindset and accepts more challenges. You are a conscious being; your thoughts and ideas are conscious. Consciousness strives for expression and evolution. Expression manifests in various aspects of our lives, from the clothes we wear, the shapes of our bodies, and the styles of our hair to the types of cars we drive. Though not always, there are moments when we yearn for something more, seeking to expand the boundaries of our self-expression. Look at the trees around you; they still grow no matter how often they are cut or trimmed. When you believe something is true, willpower ignites strength and courage. It fights for its existence. Even if your beliefs are not necessarily true, willpower still ignites strength and courage, fighting for existence.

For most of us, our beliefs fight for existence daily through pain. Some things that propel us are that we want our voices heard, and we use words to express our pain and actions to demonstrate how the pain makes us feel. But what and who are we fighting? Is it someone else, or is it an accepted belief that generates a feeling? And what if the emotion you feel is a universal language or law that supports the manifestation of the energy and attention you give to it?

Could some people get caught up as I did by giving energy and attention to the things I did not know I did not want? Igniting courage and strength to victimhood and weakness, not knowing I was keeping it alive? I was not aware that my belief was the fuel in the car; the car doesn't care where you are going as long as it has enough energy to get you from point A to point B. I gave my beliefs enough energy to repeat and reproduce themselves like the process of mitosis.

Being unaware makes me a perfect candidate to be entirely under the influence of emotional suffering.

Every feeling I felt I believed was true, and it was; there is no denying that based on my understanding at the time. Whenever I am faced with an emotion, I take on that identity of what I felt. Sometimes, that feeling kept me in a cycle for days, weeks, and even months. I was unaware of my emotional patterns because I lacked self-awareness. Being unaware makes me a perfect candidate to be entirely under the influence of emotional suffering.

Doing the same thing repeatedly strengthens your confidence and claims more ground. We have often heard the term deep-rooted belief. Yes, it is covered under many layers. Think of planting a tree. The seed is an idea or a belief. The seed is covered under the soil in darkness. Every day, you water the seed, and eventually, it starts making its way out of the ground and expressing itself. Showing the world who it is. It is the same with a belief; the more you hear about something, the more it takes that form and becomes: my deep-rooted beliefs, ideas, thoughts, and imagination of emotional suffering took precedence in my life. This led to unhealthy relationships made up of toxic behaviors, communication barriers, distorted self-images, and running with narratives correlated to my pain. This perfect demonstration can be understood using the cause-and-effect universal law theory. We will get more into that later.

As I stood at the window watching my daughter sleep, all I could think of was how we were victims of this crime. My silent gaze wandered and steered. I quickly snapped out of my glaze and returned to the living room and my chair. I was nervous and petrified, embracing every second. What are you going to ask me next, I thought. Should I be acting nervous? I thought to myself. Should I act as if I am strong, as if I got it together? I don't know, I said to myself. Just be yourself, but I don't want to be myself; I want this to disappear. I did not know what I wanted except to escape the uncomfortable feeling I was experiencing.

Seated and anxiously awaiting answers, I noticed no one was posing questions to me. Instead, they chatted and spoke on their phones and talked to each other. I could not shake the feeling that they were keeping something from me, perhaps a development in the search for my husband. Had he been located? Had they gained new insights that they had not shared? These questions consumed me, as he is my spouse, and I desperately craved any information available.

My husband and I first met at a weekly Bible study group at the home of one of the group leaders. I recall his entrance; he wore a white t-shirt, blue jean shorts, and a wooden cross adorned his neck. Although his outfit was okay, his shoes were a bit worn. At that time, I was not seeking a relationship, as I was seeing someone else, and I had never considered dating a white guy. He arrived late to the meeting, but when he walked in, he respectfully greeted us and apologized for his tardiness. We allowed him to join us, and the meeting proceeded as usual. As the session drew close, we warmly welcomed him, even inviting him to our Sunday service. And sure enough, he showed up the following Sunday.

As I mentioned, I was dating someone else when I met my husband, and I was not looking for a relationship. He continued to attend our Sunday services for several months and even started volunteering and assisting with various tasks around the church. As time went by, we became friends and fellow churchgoers. He struck me as a reserved individual who did not speak much but was courteous. I did notice that my future husband always chose to sit behind me during church services, but I did not take it as a sign of anything other than his preference for that spot. On the other hand, I was blessed with two well-rounded buttocks that may have caught a few wandering eyes, but that could just be my perspective!

We were both around the same age, so we tended to have more things in common to talk about. One evening at our weekly bible study meeting, our leader announced, "It's that time of the year again for our annual banquet."

Everyone was so excited! Because they got to dress up, look fancy, take pictures, and, most of all, have fun. Since I had ended the relationship with my boyfriend, I decided to sit that one out because I did not want to be a loner or a plus one at the banquet. Everyone talked about what they would wear and who they would go to the banquet with, while I sat, listened and even gave input on what they should wear and what hairstyle they should get. Someone suggested that my soon-to-be husband and I should go together. I thought, *What gave them that idea?*

He was sitting three chairs away from me. Hence, he turned and said, "Only if she pays for the ticket."

I scrunched my face, gave a curious look, and thought, *How rude of him to say that. I did not even propose the idea or think of hanging out with him.* The proposal caught me off guard because it never really crossed my mind to go out on a date with him, even though we were friends. We all laughed it off and went our separate ways.

The next day, I got a call from my leader. She said my husband had bought me a ticket for the banquet and wanted to know what color dress I would wear. I was speechless! At first, I thought, *Why would he buy me a ticket? Was it out of pity? Or was he persuaded by someone to take me?* I reluctantly remembered his response the night before, which offended me. How confused was I? Was this guy giving me mixed signals? My mind ran rampant with contemplations. But I responded that I would go to the banquet with him. I did not have a dress because I had not planned to attend the banquet that year. But since he offered to take me to the banquet, I knew I needed to shop for a dress.

During childhood, I was often scrutinized for my knock-knees and called names like "Capital K." Body shaming was brutal for me; not only were my knees knocked, but I also struggled with weight as well. I was so skinny that they used to call me "chicken." Growing up in Jamaica, being considered overweight is a compliment, particularly if you have lighter skin. They used to call slim women "mauger gal" while heavier women were called "sexy browning" (in Jamaican patois). When migrating to the United States, body image is reversed; everyone wants to be skinny.

Later that week, I wore a stunning bright green dress with a black mesh overlay on the green fabric. It was the perfect outfit for a night out in town. I informed him about my dress, and to my surprise, he showed up wearing a bright green tie and presented me with a beautiful green and white flower corsage for my hand. As we walked into the banquet hall together, all eyes were on us. We decided to sit with our peers at the same table, and while enjoying the delicious meal, he asked me about my interests. When I mentioned my love for movies, he suggested that we catch a movie the following weekend, to which I happily agreed; that evening marked the beginning of our relationship.

We enjoyed spending time with each other and sharing our family backgrounds and upbringing. I grew up in the mountains, so I did not have much street exposure, while he grew up in the city and had more street smarts. Whenever we went out together, I would make excuses to leave early because I had to wake up early for my paper route job. He only knew about my retail job working at Target, not my paper route job. I did not tell him about the paper route because of hidden pride, or I thought he might judge me. My schedule was so packed back then I did not have time to share. I would wake up at 2 a.m. to wrap newspapers and deliver them before heading to my other job--then to classes at the community college in the evening!

It was not long before he asked why I had to go home so early after our dates. So, I told him about the paper route. He was perplexed about why I had said nothing before. I was embarrassed about the paper route and thought that he would judge me, but that was all in my head. The following morning, he showed up at my door, ready to go with me and throw my papers. I could not understand why he would leave his warm bed to throw newspapers with me. But nothing I said stopped him. I remember I had to go on a mission trip to Nicaragua with my church, and he offered to throw my route the entire week I was gone. How sweet of him to do this for me. We had so many great moments in the wee of the morning, just us on the road in the dark. He came daily with me until I quit the paper route about a year later.

"Are you okay, Mrs. Harrington?" the police officer, asked.

"Yes, I am," I replied, "but please tell me what is happening. Did you guys hear anything about his whereabouts?"

"No, nothing as yet," he answered. "But we still have some more questions for you. Is that okay, Mrs. Harrington?"

"Yes, that's okay. But first, can I go check on my daughter?"

"Of course," he said.

I got up from the little seat in the corner and went into the bedroom to check on my baby as she gracefully slept through the turmoil. I just momentarily felt alone again; I wanted to punch the wall. I wanted to scream. I wanted someone to hold me. I was so afraid. I knew I needed someone else with me here. No one knew what was going on. I needed some emotional support, anyone. I could not bear this alone. This is too much, I thought, but with my back against the wall, tears in my eyes, and the feeling of heartbreak, I found myself just being present and simply focusing on the next thing and taking it moment by moment.

The window had parallel glass, and I opened the window by turning the crank to see the cars passing on the street from where I was sitting. In the room where I was sitting, two black leather sofas and a centerpiece were in the middle. The two end tables had the police officer's paperwork. The room was small for ten people but big enough for three people, one bedroom, one bathroom, and a kitchen big enough for my little family. It was about 3 p.m. with no sign of my husband, phone call, or explanation. It felt like time was moving fast because the lions were rumbling in my stomach, but food was the last thing on my mind.

Here I was, waiting anxiously and scared while trying to be brave.

"How much longer?" I asked because I wanted to leave the house and go to my parents. The officers told me they did not have an estimated time for me and that I needed to sit tight and wait.

It is one thing to wait when you know what you are waiting for. It is another beast when you do not see or understand what you are waiting for, and you are praying for the best outcome. But I had to ask life some questions while I was waiting. With my head held down, I unleashed these questions to myself.

"Fear, where did you come from?"

"Worry, who sent you?"

"Shame; why are you trying to take me out?'

"Current situation, I have done nothing wrong."

"Why am I your victim? The moment I found something worth loving that became mine, here you go, taking it away."

"Life, what else can I do to prove I am not a bad person." (My distorted self-image).

"Regarding religion, I believe I am a faithful and devoted Christian. How can I go wrong when I have crossed all my t's and dotted all my i's?

But life kept silent, and all I could do was go through the motions. I felt all the emotions I did not want to experience but had to, whether I liked it or not.

CHAPTER FOUR:
FIGHTING A FEELING OR FIGHTING SELF?

found myself in a situation where things seemed to have hit rock bottom, and I could not have imagined anything worse. At that moment, I was left wondering, *What now? Where do I go from here? What steps do I need to take to move forward?* I was willing to do whatever it took to escape the negative emotions that had me overwhelmed.

I could not accept what had happened as something that I deserved or should endure. My sense of pride prevented me from accepting it as my reality. My past experiences had taught me how to handle conflicts and keep secrets, but this situation was too significant to hide. I never imagined facing something of this magnitude, and my denial was fueled by the belief that I was somehow different.

I'm not supposed to be in this type of situation, I thought to myself. It is one thing to keep my secrets hidden away when they're confined to closed doors, but it is an entirely different beast when they're broadcasted globally. I was struggling to accept and deal with the shame and disgrace that came with it. I also had to face abandonment, heartbreak, and regret. It was overwhelming to experience all those emotions at once, and I had to find a way to come out of it with my integrity intact and my head held high. I found myself stuck in a trench between love and hate. Love for my family, sanity, peace of mind, and pride. But I hated the exposure of the negative backlash and the shame of being seen as flawed.

It felt like every stone on the ground was thrown at me. I wanted people to stop throwing stones at me with their eyes, thoughts, and beliefs. I was getting hit from every direction, all created by my perception of the situation. My mind and body were overwhelmed, and I had to confront my feelings head-on. There was no escaping from myself; I had to endure the pain of feeling all the emotions. I did not realize then that I had created all the feelings and emotions based solely on my beliefs.

My beliefs about what should or should not have happened. My belief about what others thought of us. My belief about what the future might look like. My beliefs about what I thought was happening at that time. My beliefs of expectation from my husband. My belief about the law. My belief about breaking the rules. My belief about family. My belief about myself.

We advise others on handling certain situations based on what we believe we would do in their place at the time, not necessarily because we have experienced the same thing. There is nothing wrong with learning from others' mistakes and using them to guide us; however, I realized that personal experience is the best teacher you can ever ask for.

If I had not experienced the absence of self-love, I would not understand the importance of loving myself.

The experiences I had in my life did not provide answers while going through the process. Maybe because I was not looking for answers. Instead, I was looking to blame. Time has, however, become the great revealer of the answers.

Fear, Where Did You Come From?

Fear is a belief. My belief in fear kept me a prisoner in my mind for many years. It was the battle between my perceptions and deep-rooted beliefs. It took me quite some time to understand that my belief in fear kept fear alive. I consistently affirmed all the what-ifs I did not want, the things I told myself I was worried about—trying to escape the expectations and irrational thinking. That storyline kept me committed and loyal to fear. I did not understand that fear is neutral, just like anything else; all fear needed was my time and attention to activate its force. It is only when someone believes in whatever is presented as something they do not want that fear is manifested. Each person's interpretation is different; two people can experience the same thing, but the level of fear experienced is based on personal belief.

All fear needs are time and attention to survive. Two people can hear the same news of something deadly. One can activate fear by giving it attention, and the other can deactivate fear by not giving attention. Fear is generational, passing down through friends, family, and social environment. No one is exempt from fear. Even as a child, we were told not to do this or that "or else." The *or else* insinuated fear of the consequence. I, too, became a carrier of fear. Accepting the belief in fear of my thoughts and emotions ultimately helped to shape my actions and decision-making.

I can remember my first experience of fear. My innocents were taken through sexual abuse, and I created a sensation to associate what I encountered with a specific feeling. I did not have the understanding that my emotions were my creation. I am not addressing the other person's action; I am sharing how that experience affected the creation of my emotional pain and how I interpreted and carried those feelings for many years. As an adult, I was still affected by those feelings I created as a child, not knowing that those emotions were still operating in my everyday life.

Understand that whatever traumatic event happens to me, right or wrong, I am the creator of the feeling and emotion based on my perception of that situation. It feels better to say, "You did this to me." But even if the person says, "I am sorry" and genuinely regrets what happened, it is still up to me to recreate or transform those first feelings and emotions and the energy given to them--generating a better feeling that would support the life I want to live.

I did not have strong family support to protect me, which made me an easy target. I did not have professional help, such as a counselor or therapist, to help me understand my mental suffering. I did not even know that my cognitive development was limited. Therefore, I learned early to wear different masks to blend in with my surroundings. The act was so second-nature that I did not even know they were masks. I would pretend to look and feel comfortable in my skin. But I was scared and worried, and I felt powerless. I told myself I was strong, so I showed up in the world with a strong front but a weakness inside, and I thought that would heal my wounds. My misconception of what healing looks like is more common than you might imagine.

I WAS STILL SCARED when I met my husband, but playing the courageous woman role. It was the first time someone made me feel safe, and I felt I could be myself with him and finally live the righteous life God wanted for me. I did not have to show my strength because he became my strength. That did not last long before my safety was threatened when things took a turn. I was still hiding even though I had found a sense of security in my husband. My security was temporary. Some people call it the honeymoon phase. I was married but remained loyal to fear's many years of threats and tactics deep within, buried under my new happy life without awareness.

Fear shows up as many things, like worry, disappointments, excuses, and shame. I gave all of these emotions time and attention. Looking back over my life, I realize that I served in fear. I lived the whole first part of my life in fear. I feared going to hell, so I did my best to serve God as I was taught. Not realizing that I was already living in hell in my mind. I feared making mistakes; I feared getting hurt and hurt again. But mistakes help us learn and grow. I feared being judged by others, but, in reality, it was my own belief about what I *thought* others were thinking. I feared not having financial support. But it was because I was not willing to sacrifice for what I wanted. I feared not having a career. Because I believed in the narrative that my skin color is the great determiner. I feared having my family fall apart because of my past fear of not having a family growing up. I feared being criticized for my experiences and viewpoints because people talk about others with different opinions. Every fear thought I had was laced with suspicion, past programming even amid my faith.

You may be saying, woman, "Where was your faith?" My faith never left me. It was right there, but my fears were more potent and profound and had the advantage of developing stronger before I knew how to believe in myself. To visually explain where my faith was, think

What you focus on the most magnifies.

of two dogs chained up, one called light and the other darkness. Which one of the dogs will outlive the other? If you said light, you are wrong; it is the one you feed the most. I learned how to believe in fear before I learned how to believe in myself. What you focus on the most magnifies. In Jamaica, we often say, "You always turn a molehill into a mountain" emphasizing making a big deal out of a small thing. Or, in my case, using up all my mental capital to invest in a belief that would not give me a more profitable return. I was unaware that what I was affirming was killing, stealing, and destroying my present and possibly my future.

I became a people pleaser, hoping for safety, acceptance, and validation. Getting married gave me a sense of security and acceptance but not validation. I still had trust issues, and even though I tried to convince myself otherwise, I did. My marriage allowed me to step into another arena accompanied by my past traumas, and I believed this was the answer. I needed proof that I could trust and open my heart fully. When I got married, I did not admit what I mentioned as my truth because I convinced myself that if that were the case, I was questioning my loyalty and love to my husband. Therefore, I was left to wonder and shift what was pure and what was not. The irony was that I was looking for these things from my husband when I should have been looking inside myself. I questioned his commitment to using societal weapons of mass destruction that break apart most relationships, and that is EXPECTATIONS.

Both women and men face specific expectations based on their gender. Typically, women are expected to be caregivers and nurturers, while men are often seen as protectors and providers. Additionally, within a relationship, there are further expectations. For example, I once expected my husband to embody certain qualities that would make me feel loved. I realized, however, that feeling loved was something only I could achieve for myself, not something that could be fulfilled by marriage alone.

My environment shaped my fears and faith. During my childhood, I heard the word "no" frequently, but my curious nature pushed me to challenge those restrictions. While some "nos" were helpful, others proved unhelpful. I was also told I needed to be saved, as I was considered a sinner. These messages created a narrative for a negative self-image, and I spent most of my life trying to redeem myself and save my soul.

But what was my crime? Was it being born? Was it the wrong skin color? Was it the mistaken geolocation? A young child's mind is like a sponge, quickly soaking up water spilled on the ground. My mind was the sponge; the water was the words and phrases, verbal or non-verbal communication. As a child, I did not have the intelligence to differentiate metaphorical storytelling, so I took most of what I heard literally.

From the moment I was born, I became an observer, actively gathering and storing data from various sources such as my environment, culture, traditions, religion, social settings, and mass media marketing. I learned how to fear, worry, stress, laugh, hope, give, and be reasonable based on how it was presented to me in my surroundings. As a new member of society, I naturally wanted to fit in and demonstrate what I had learned and could do. This is typical behavior for human evolution.

Once I had collected the data, I processed and transcribed the information, incorporating my perceptions and beliefs. Through repeated practice and observation, certain behaviors and beliefs became my norm, shaping my unique personality with deep-rooted convictions.

I am like a picture on the wall in my frame. Everyone around me is also like a picture in their frames. Now, if you close your eyes, all you see is a blank canvas. The blank canvas is all the same. The canvas represents us as humans, and we are all a part of the universe. Each frame is made of different conditioning and personal environments. The colors on the canvas are also different; just like the color of our lives, our experiences create different strokes, curved lines, and circles. The thread that stitches the fabric of the canvas connects surrounding units like our families and friends. The same unit connects race, religion, politics, and social status.

Some frames stay intact, while others fall apart, get broken, tossed aside, or destroyed. The frame's condition can be overlooked if broken, smashed, or smudged. What matters to the viewer is if the picture is still visible. A good artist can enhance the colors of a painting over the years to keep the pictures looking good. Ensuring the picture looks like what our environment welcomes. However, a great artist can recreate an image and change the frame to what they want. The purpose of the painting is for the artist to look at his/her image when it is complete and say, "Well done. I am pleased with the work I did. I love what I see and what I have created."

We are all artists. We are painting our images or having someone else paint our pictures for us. It all depends on what the artist can visualize in their mind. Daily, I painted my beliefs, perceptions, ideas, and moral standards. They say a picture is worth a thousand words. Take a minute and look at a picture of yourself, then write down a thousand words. These words may encompass your journey from what you remember growing up to where you are now: the ups, the downs, the lessons, the hardships, and the victories. I am sure you can come up with a thousand words.

Growing up, I first learned to color and draw stick man figures. I was taught to color within the lines. I tried my best to color within the lines, but sometimes, my impatience got the best of me, leading me to color outside the lines and even on top of other colors. I just wanted to get it over with and move on to something more fun. I guess I was not a patient child. Instant gratification was the culprit, but I just wanted to get it done to show the teacher that I had done it. "What's next?"

The older I got, the better I became at understanding coloring. But it still was not my thing. I liked connecting numbers to form images. That was more satisfying for me. I love connecting the dots but hated coloring the pictures after they were formed. I guess I did not like the images I saw. I did not want to color them because I already knew and felt what they looked like. And I did not want to be judged on my coloring skills. I carried that mentality throughout my adult life, building the image of my perception of reality, what I think it should look like rather than what it is currently. I did not want the world to see what was on my mind, thoughts, and beliefs.

My images had mental, sexual, and emotional abuse. The shame of being criticized paralyzed my coloring skills. It eventually stopped my creativity from flowing freely. I did not have a role model or leader to help me practice or try to work on my skills. Instead, I hid, held back my craft, and buried my attention in the running from shame. Shame was an image I had that I did not know how to face or conquer. I became the victim, and everything that was said was not for me. No one else around me was coloring shame. Everyone seemed to be running and hiding.

It is hard enough not to want to paint your mess, but even worse when you have to cover it with the phrase "you should." *You should look like that. You should act like that. You should be like that.* Somewhere between the image of myself in my head and the "you should," I got lost. Who am I again? Am I still the little girl who wants to color her picture the way she wants to but is too afraid to color outside the lines? Or am I the girl culturally conditioned to be in the "you should frame"? Am I a good artist, or am I a great artist?

CHAPTER FIVE:
WHY OWE YOU?

Y-O-U

Why owe you my future self? I said to my past.

Why owe you my true acceptance? I said to my fears of being judged.

Why owe you my freedom? I said to the stigma of shame.

Why owe you my health? I said to the unhealthy lifestyle.

Why owe you my wealth? I said to the poverty mindset.

Why owe you my joy and happiness? I said to the unhealthy emotions.

Who are you again? I am my best advocate, deliverer, healer, and giver of life. I permitted myself to thrive, flourish, spread my wings, paint the picture I want to look at, smile, and say, "Well done. I am pleased; I am proud of the woman I am becoming."

Today, people carry cultural narratives, images, and mindsets they have never experienced. But it is because of the thread that stitches the fabric of their culture and tradition, religion, race, and social settings. They believe in the culture's fear, stress, mental suffering, victories, and joy. Accepting the actual narrative creates a belief that will fight for its existence. Cultural conditioning gives you the resources and quick data to paint the same picture of yourself without the awareness that you are a blank canvas replicating the same ideas, thoughts, and beliefs to run rapidly in your mind, letting them become your reality. Cultural conditioning is good if what is being passed down adds value to the next generation.

But, although the thread that stitches the fabric is the same, the images can be different. To *be* different requires you to *do* differently. Think about what you want to see when you look at your picture. Will you say, "Well done?" Or will you say, "I have so many regrets? Did I choose my tools, or did my cultural conditioning choose them for me? Was I creative, or was I surviving?" Whichever answer you give yourself, just remember it is not your fault. You did nothing wrong. You only know what you know. You do not know what you do not know. You did not know because you were not exposed. But now that you know, the question now is, what will you do about it?

Sirens and Guns

At the house, with all the chattering and sirens, police uniforms, guns, flashlights, and handcuffs jiggling. I was in a situation I never thought would be my reality in a million years. At this time, I still had the identity of the learned behavior of shame, fear, worry, and other emotional pain. Facing the truth of the crime committed by my husband was more significant than my fears. The foundation of our life was shaken, which we thought we had worked so hard on building. The feeling of being abandoned again was surfacing, and I could not control it. It felt like a continuous cycle that kept coming back to haunt me. The only difference was the storyline and the scene. Have you ever felt like your secret has been exposed, leaving an awful feeling inside your gut? Wishing and hoping to change the outcome to something you can tolerate more.

While looking through the window, I saw a helicopter flying over my area. I was sure it was connected to what was going on in my house. The sound of the helicopter made the scene more of a highly intense reality to me. Now, it is a search for the Dappa Bandit. You could hear the sound getting louder and louder as it got closer to my house. It was like I was lost in space. I did not know precisely what the officers were conversing over and the main reason for the helicopter. Did someone see him? Are they tracking him, or was it just a random search to find him? No one told me any specific details; I was left to wonder about my regrets and disappointment. All I could think of was, "Shit; things were getting real." You could see the neighbors looking out and people passing by, wondering what was happening. I did not know what they knew, nor did I care what they thought.

I got up from where I was sitting and went to the bathroom, only to find myself on the floor, wailing and sobbing. Right then and there, I told myself, Stephanie, you have to be strong. Hold your head up and be brave, especially for your daughter. When I looked in the mirror at myself talking, it sounded encouraging. It gave me a boost of courage, but as I stood there and looked myself in the eyes, it broke me down, and I started crying. Up and down my chest went. Throw me a washcloth, maybe a towel. I am flooding the bathroom with my tears.

Everyone watching has a question. They say that questions were made to ask, but only some people want answers. Even life itself keeps quiet at times. Not all questions get comfortable answers.

Nevertheless, questions do serve their purpose. It took me a long time to adapt to the mentality of questioning everything. If I had asked more questions, I would have saved myself a lot of headaches and stress rather than creating more imagination and playing mind games. Mind games are a softening mechanism that helps shield my discomfort. But what exactly are mind games? Some say "playing hard to get," especially in the early dating stage, using manipulation to get my way, like sending mixed signals or empty threats.

Instead of asking questions, I would assume the answer and then project my assumption onto my husband as if it were his. It may have sounded like:

"You know you are not happy. Just admit it." **Let me break this down.**

"You know." **I am projecting my feelings onto him to accept.**

"You are not happy." **I am questioning his feelings for my security.**

"Just admit it." **I am softening the blow for myself because I haven't accepted that he is just happy with me.**

My mind games originated from my past, questioning the future and being unable to accept the present. It is a selfish act that can cause a lot of unrest in romantic relationships, acquaintanceships, work relationships, and even teacher/student relationships. Fear, resentment, and disappointment fueled the mind game energy, which gave me room to dance with my tactics. This action was a created survival skill. The motive was never to harm or hurt anyone but to feel security. This was my way of protecting my feelings and answering my what-ifs questions. I did not know that what I was doing was creating internal conflict with our bond. The energy I was sending out was insecurity, low self-esteem, and the belief that I was not lovable.

The first scripture my husband quoted me over the phone while we were dating is 1 Corinthians 13, which talks about love being embodied and demonstrated through patience & kindness, not harming, and so on. But the embodiment was not for me; at that time, I believed it was for him to be that for me. It took years to understand that I needed to be patient with myself, be kind to myself, and not do things to harm myself. In doing so, I then understood how to be patient with others and be kind to others. You cannot give what you do not have yourself; anything given not from abundance is a loan or transactional.

The day before my husband asked me to marry him, we went to my parent's house, and he pulled my dad aside and asked him if he could have his daughter's hand in marriage. From across the room, I could sense something going on. They both looked nervous, and my dad could not get the smile off his face. His eyes lit up, and his cheeks rose to the side, making me want to ask what's happening with him.

Later that night, my dad took me outside and said, "Your guy, he asked me for your hand in marriage."

I quickly asked, "What did you say?"

He replied, "I told him, 'Yes, if that's what you guys want to do.'"

It felt like fireworks going off in my head and like butterflies in my stomach. Any new chapter for anyone can be scary. I allowed my heart to lead the way; my mind and body followed. Within less than a year of dating, we got engaged.

Families are the roots of connection that stem from the same tree. Trees are connected underground through a mycorrhizal network. This connection transfers water, nitrogen, carbon, and other minerals. It is like a World Wide Web under the ground. It is the same with families. They are the bedrock of our communities. What holds a family together is love, respect, and honor. Family supports each other and shares in your joy and suffering. Having shared values supersedes what breaks families apart.

Growing up, my Jamaican culture taught me to keep our business at home and keep our problems private from others. There is evidence that if you go against this, there will be repercussions, like gossip, backbiting, slander, and quarrels. The idea is to keep the threat away from you and your family.

Having the "Bandit" broadcasting all over the globe was a threat to me. It was a threat to my beliefs, values, and cultural norms. Never bleed so the world can see you; instead, you must hide it. We have incorporated creative ways to cover our shame, pain, and indifference. There are some phrases that you might be familiar with, like:

"You will bring nothing but disgrace and embarrassment to our house."

"Whatever goes on in this house stays in this house."

"You better not say anything."

"Nobody can know this."

"What a shame."

My usual approach was always to do what I believed was the norm, which meant doing whatever possible to make my surroundings feel less threatening. I learned to hide well, push my troubles under a rug, and pretend to be strong. But what is strength? Is strength holding on to a belief even if that belief is not serving your immediate circumstance? Or is it letting that belief go amidst everyone's eyes on you and feeling like you are going against all the odds, but you do it anyway? This seems more like strength and courage to me.

Our environment influences our mental development. We are like aliens in a new world. Of course, we will do what makes us feel accepted and, or, you can say, fit in. So, if it is customary in your culture to not bleed or show any signs of adversity, going against what your culture believes is expected will be considered an embarrassment because "you should" know better. It is one thing to create a pair of eyes to see the stigma of shame, but it is another beast when you uphold that same belief.

What Exactly is Shame?

Shame is a feeling of remorse or disgrace resulting from doing something wrong or failing to meet certain expectations. It is often accompanied by embarrassment and self-loathing, leading to feelings of inadequacy and low self-esteem.

Shame can be a normal and healthy emotion that helps us recognize when we have made mistakes and motivates us to make amends and move on with our lives. Excessive or prolonged shame can be harmful, leading to negative self-perception and unhealthy coping mechanisms such as avoidance or self-destructive behaviors.

On the day of the robbery, I did not experience shame as such. Instead, I was more concerned about my husband's safety than anything else. The feeling of shame emerged later when I began thinking about what had happened. I started to worry about what others might think and say behind my back. I was concerned about losing my friends, being judged harshly, being laughed at, and damaging my reputation. These thoughts gave rise to feelings of shame.

People process their experiences differently, and there is no one-size-fits-all approach to handling them. For instance, how I respond to a specific situation might differ from how someone else would respond to a similar situation. Some individuals might experience feelings of shame immediately, while others may not.

My alter ego tends to fade away during high-intensity situations, and my higher self takes charge. As a result, my response to the situation might be different from how I would react under normal circumstances. Nonetheless, it is essential to recognize that people process their experiences uniquely, and there is no right or wrong way to do so.

I interviewed some of my fellow islanders with similar cultural conditioning backgrounds of shame and fear. They explained what shame meant to them, and here was their response.

It makes them feel like outcasts. Being labeled an outcast carries emotional pain that no one willingly wants to bear. The fight then goes inward with questions of why you cannot be understood or accepted.

They do not like it when people talk about them. It can stir anger and possibly cause them to want to harm someone physically.

It hurts severely to look into the eyes of others, so people avoid eye contact at all costs. This behavior can create mental isolation.

They are afraid of the spotlight; too much unhealthy attention can damage their reputation.

They do not want people to treat them differently. They do not like to be judged.

They can lose the respect of the people, especially if they are public figures.

Upon conducting several interviews, I realized that the responses I received were simply regurgitated ideas and beliefs ingrained in us through conditioning. As we internalize these beliefs, they become a part of us, and we become carriers of the stigma of shame. The more we believe in shame, the more we accept it as our own, leading to the absence of vulnerability and a predominance of judgment. In such a scenario, nobody wants to be judged. Living a comfortable lie is much easier than confronting the uncomfortable truth.

Living a comfortable lie is much easier than confronting the uncomfortable truth.

It is a must to make mistakes. How else are we going to evolve? There was a time when I was too afraid to take risks. Or even entertain the idea of stepping out of my comfort zone and trying anything new. A comfort zone that was hard for me to step out of was the narrative of "waiting." I was waiting for a rescuer, a vindicator, a deliverer to come and show up for me in a great way. My waiting mindset caused me to look outside of myself instead of inside myself. Breaking free from waiting caused much unrest and unanswered questions that angered an act of revenge. Revenge, however, is another form of accepting another narrative and wearing its label. This label meant someone needed to take the blame for my pain and everyone else around me who was still waiting. This was my mismark, the creative experience that allowed me the exposure I needed to evolve to love. I searched for meaning back then, but all I could find was a broken, hurting child asking life, "Why me?" Shame was not gentle with me in my earlier years, but it showed me why it had to be me as I got older.

Instead of taking on the victim's role, I took the challenger role and challenged my belief about what and why I uphold a particular narrative. This challenger role was not easy; it did not happen without a mental fight. To understand my battle, I started with questions. I would ask myself questions like, *When did I first believe this? Is this belief serving me now or hurting me? What would happen if I let this belief go?*

Shame is a belief in a feeling, a learned behavior that can be unlearned. There are only two sides to it: above or under its influence. Under shame's influence, it could mean accepting the feeling and the narrative and expressing its existence. Above shame's influence could mean understanding that you are a conductor with a choice. The feelings or thoughts that flood your mind and body do not define you. I was so caught up with being identified that I spent the majority of my life trying to show who I was *not* while not knowing who I *was*. By definition, identity is the key to all marketing strategies. Which label am I led to believe I am, and whose label am I willing to wear? Is it shame, fear, victimhood, the oppressed, poverty, insecurities, low self-esteem, ignorance, stress, the minority, wealthy, healthy, happy, prosperous, or the 1% or 99% the list goes on?

I can remember, when I was thirteen years old, wondering where I came from before I was born. This little girl had a lot of questions. If you were the Creator of this little girl, you would understand the intricate complexities of her being. You would not be concerned with cultural, traditional, religious, or social backgrounds but rather her reactions to various life experiences. You would observe how she coped with pain, made sacrifices, found happiness, and dealt with stress. You would notice how she loved, shared, and gave of herself and others and her ability to understand and be understood. None of her choices or actions would be deemed right or wrong, only what she deemed best for herself. From your perspective as the observer, she would be perfect.

During this observation exercise, picture yourself being observed and embrace your perfection for thirty seconds. Then, try to imagine someone who has hurt or caused discomfort in your life, not from your viewpoint, but as an observer looking down on that person. The Creator can see beyond the surface layers that shape the little girl's mindset, actions, and habits, as well as, what limits her.

We often focus on the superficial surface of things, such as scratches, cracks, marks, or the fading paint color. I taught myself to hide well to cover up the scars, scratches, and cracks because the way I see others is the way I judge myself. Even though I learned that Jesus showed his scars, I still hid mine. At that time, I never truly understood what this teaching meant.

Embracing your perfection detaches all aspects of identity's power and influence. Letting go of shame is embracing your perfection. Hiding behind shame is taking on a commercialized identity.

CHAPTER SIX:
DOES AGE CONSIDER MATURITY?

My heart was going ba-boom ba-boom. I could feel my chest echoing as it moved up and down. The tips of my fingers were tingling, the palms of my hands sweating, my mind racing with what-if scenarios. Am I experiencing symptoms of a panic attack or a heart attack? I don't know. I find myself saying, "Oh, my God, no," repeatedly. I felt afraid; my hands were shaking. The feeling was overwhelming as my emotions were projecting and transcribing, switching from thoughts and feelings to thoughts and sensations.

I held many people responsible for knowing and doing better, especially older ones. But as I got older, I realized that age is just a number.

A person's age tells the story of the time a person lived. Age is measured in years, days, and minutes. What age does not tell is a person's mental and emotional maturity level. There are three basic maturity types: biological, cognitive, and emotional. Biological maturity is considered physical growth from a baby to a teen stage and then to adulthood, like a plant turning into a tree. Emotional and mental maturity involves being able to recognize and manage one's own emotions, as well as, being able to understand and empathize with others. It also involves communicating effectively, setting and achieving goals, making responsible decisions, developing better-coping skills, and developing critical thinking skills.

When the robbery occurred, we were both twenty-seven years old. If a personality assessment were to gauge my level of maturity, it would likely indicate that I excel at completing physical tasks. Since childhood, I have been accustomed to performing household chores and caring for others. I became proficient in cooking by the age of twelve. By the time I got married, I had managed multiple jobs to support my family while ensuring bills were paid and other domestic duties were attended to. In essence, I had learned to survive.

Regarding mental maturity, the assessment would likely indicate that I now understand the need to put aside childish things and behave like an adult. At that time, though, this meant projecting an image of having everything under control and using language that reinforced my maturity without presenting any facts to support my arguments.

Regarding emotional maturity, the assessment suggests that my emotions heavily influenced me and that I often acted impulsively without being aware of their control over me.

My physical, mental, and emotional maturation is all influenced by my perceptions. The mind grows whatever is planted inside of it. If you believe your age gives you maturity, then that is what you will exhibit and proudly model.

My mother and I have had many disagreements throughout the years, and we've had plenty of opportunities to practice our communication skills. When I was younger, I thought I knew everything, and my mother would often end our conversations by saying, "Because I am your mother." This phrase always bothered me because it seemed like she was using her title to shut down the conversation, even if it had nothing to do with her role as a mother.

Unfortunately, my mother had a habit of waiting to respond rather than listening to understand. This created one-sided conversations that frustrated me. It all boils down to a lack of mental and emotional maturity on both our parts. To be clear,

Age and title should not be the only factors determining the authority level in a conversation or relationship.

passing down wisdom or sharing life experiences is not bad. Rather, age and title should not be the only factors determining the authority level in a conversation or relationship.

I made the mistake of relying on my title and age to establish dominance in my marriage, ultimately hindering our communication ability. Instead of embodying the role of a true partner and friend to my husband, I often asserted my authority by saying things like "because I'm your wife." It was not until a family member asked me if we were friends that I realized how much I had focused on my title instead of fulfilling it. I had been so focused on being what I believed a wife should be that I forgot to be my husband's friend and see him for who he was.

To maintain control, I became the "marriage police," enforcing rules and dictating what a husband should be, even though I never had or saw what a real husband should be. This behavior frustrated my husband, and I soon realized that my definitions of these roles were based on societal conditioning and personal perception rather than actual understanding. I would often compare my husband to other men I saw in leadership roles at church, assuming that they were all perfect and that he should be like them. I failed to realize that these men were only presenting their best selves on Sundays, and I was creating an unrealistic standard for my husband to meet.

Letting go of my need for control and authority was against the understanding of what true allowance is. Ultimately, I learned that an essential aspect of any relationship is seeing and accepting the other person for who they are without imposing our expectations or societal norms.

Looking back, I realize how immature and naive I was in the early stages of building a life with my husband. Instead of using our materials and tools to construct our foundation, I relied heavily on the ideas and opinions of others, particularly those in positions of influence. I was easily swayed by people in suits, assuming that their appearance alone made them trustworthy and knowledgeable. But where did these ideas come from? Upon reflection, I recognized that my cultural upbringing emphasized respect for elders and authority figures, influencing my perception of what a "real man" should look and act like.

This reliance on external sources of authority meant I needed a greater understanding of the men around me. Without knowing intimately about their struggles or seeing them as real people rather than just a polished presentation, I formed opinions based on my perception rather than facts.

As my husband and I faced challenges building our foundation, I realized how much I had to learn. He was much more open-minded, mature, and realistic than I was while clinging to childish ideas. I realized I needed to let go of my dependence on external sources and rely more on my experiences and instincts to build a strong foundation for our life together.

I have witnessed numerous relationships and marriages fall apart due to immaturity and a lack of knowledge. Unfortunately, I was guilty of the same behavior. I became fixated on comparing my husband to the men in the pulpit. I gave them more respect than the man I had married. My misguided belief was that I was also honoring God by honoring these men.

Most of my actions were geared towards what I believed was proving my devotion to God, and I placed more weight on the words of a pastor or spiritual leader than on my husband's. In doing so, I failed to recognize the importance of valuing and respecting the man I had committed to spending my life with. My misplaced priorities could have caused irreparable harm to our relationship if I had not realized the error of my ways. You may ask, "Is robbing a bank irreparable?" My confession is not about the actions of my husband or even the molester, but rather my perception and state of mind that was leading me to the path of damnation.

I vividly recall a neighbor who prided herself on being very spiritual. When her pastor instructed her to kick her husband out of the house, she obeyed without question. She did so because he had chosen to attend a different church. I have also seen pastors call men to the altar during services and proclaim that God had commanded them to do . . . (whatever the wife had told the pastor secretly). In such cases, the wife would feel elated because it would be good if God had said it.

This behavior is widely accepted, and I, too, fell victim to its allure and attempted to apply it in my marriage. My husband, however, was not receptive to it and often asked me, "Why?" When I answered, he would ask, "Why?" again.

He was not questioning me because he did not understand my viewpoint; instead, he was helping me to challenge my ideology. Was I thinking for myself, or was I blindly following the views of others? Did I even understand the reasoning behind my beliefs? The answer was *no*, but I believed that since I was old enough to be married and have a child, I must have been mature enough to make sound decisions, as well.

It is essential to recognize that age doesn't necessarily equate to emotional maturity. Some individuals may possess emotional intelligence and self-awareness at a younger age, while others may need more time to develop these skills. Various factors, such as genetics, upbringing, life experiences, and personal traits, can influence one's emotional maturity. Regardless of age, anyone can work to improve their emotional intelligence and become more emotionally mature.

Assessing your emotional intelligence can be done in several ways. In simple terms, all you are doing is bringing awareness to your emotions. This involves paying close attention to your feelings and identifying the root cause accurately. I am not a licensed professional and simply share how I helped myself. I used to get easily angered by anything that felt like a threat to me. My response would be to do something or get someone to do or say anything that would bring back emotional stability, even in toxic situations. The truth was I was avoiding the emotional pain of the root cause without being aware of the root cause.

Another way to assess your emotional intelligence is to consider how you feel about your relationships. Do you feel you have a healthy and stable relationship with others? Are you able to communicate and empathize with others? Can you constructively resolve conflicts and approach problem-solving logically and thoughtfully, especially when facts are presented?

Seeking feedback from friends, family, or colleagues is also a helpful way to assess your emotional intelligence. They can provide valuable insights and suggestions for improvement.

Simple Tips I Used to Assess My Emotional Intelligence

I would ask myself these questions:
1. Do you have a fixed belief about how the world should be?
2. Do you feel the need to be right all the time?
3. Do you believe that you have all the answers?

These questions can help you gain self-awareness and identify any areas for growth in your emotional intelligence. If you answer yes to any of the three questions above, it signifies room for improvement and growth.

It took me a long time to learn about myself and be open to the idea that I may not have all the answers. I realized that if my mind is already made up and closed off, there is no room for new knowledge to enter. In the past, I believed that closing off my mind protected me from external influences, but it limited my ability to learn and understand new things.

My Emotional Cup

I found myself in a room with officers, and all the attention was on my family. It felt like I was reliving the trauma of a ten-year-old girl who had been sexually molested. That younger version of me was still hiding, and her emotional pain had yet to be resolved. She perceived any emotional challenge as a direct attack on her existence. Her coping mechanisms involved putting on a facade of smiles, fitting in, conforming to expectations, burying her pain, and keeping it hidden. At that moment, I felt like I could not survive the situation. Everyone in my family and beyond would discover that my husband had robbed a bank, which was too much exposure for me to bear.

Shame is a crippling and paralyzing negative emotion. Everyone experiences shame differently on a personal level. Shame is difficult to manage, and there are no specific answers. Having a greater understanding is essential to lifting the sting of shame.

Shame kept me a prisoner for a long time. It killed my dreams and sent me down a spiral cliff of mass destruction, not only to myself but to the people around me. I believe that feelings and actions affect others because we are all connected. I was a prisoner of war and, at the same time, a mighty destroyer. I would have done anything to avoid exposure; hiding felt more normal and safer. But how do you stop hiding when you do not even know you are playing hide and seek with yourself?

As a child, I loved to play hide and seek. We sometimes hid under the bed, behind doors, and in the closet; I even used to go inside the dresser drawers to hide. The goal was to avoid being found, and if it took the other person a long time to find you, you were considered the best at hiding. It gave you a sense of "I got what it takes." It is disappointing to be found quickly. You make revisions to how you could have hidden better.

Shame is like a game of hide and seek, where the only person you are hiding from is yourself. In the ancient text, God asked Adam in the garden, "Where are you?" not because He did not know where Adam was, but to help Adam reflect on his mindset and to understand why he was hiding. Life's game is played by one player, hiding from the divine within ourselves, covered with external beliefs, perceptions, and past pain. This is where I used to hide and wear various fig leaves that I would affirm and confess. It is worth noting that Adam was the one who told God that he was naked, affirming his belief in his condition. Similarly, I affirmed my shame and fears by accepting the feelings and acting out in ways connected to those emotions.

Shame is not subject to one prison. It has multiple paths to trap its prisoners. It doesn't ask questions; it gives seducing entices to follow along. I did not only follow along; I became the prosecutor, judge, and warden. Most emotions are experienced through relationships. A ship is a vessel that carries things that people make, and it also carries people. People, however, have feelings and emotions. People make up romantic relationships, work relationships, friendships, teacher/student relationships, and acquaintanceships.

A ship sets course on the ocean and anchors where it wishes to stop. A ship can get wrecked, destroyed, or even lost at sea. A ship can travel far or near depending on its purpose. A ship is of no use, though, without an ocean. My experience in life became my ocean with many emotional attachments. We construct ships to sail on the ocean and build relationships based on these emotional attachments. Like tides, waves, and ripples, our emotions can have a powerful impact. Although the ocean cannot be controlled, we can learn to observe the tides, ride the waves, and appreciate the ripples.

Women are like oceans, brimming with emotions.

Similarly, we cannot suppress our emotions but learn to recognize, understand, and appreciate them. Bad weather can ruin a good beach day, and our emotions can ruin a good day. Shame can prevent someone from seeking the help they need or cause them to sabotage their relationships rather than face their fears of vulnerability.

We all crave acceptance and belonging as social beings, but the emotions of rejection can be a painful experience. It could be as simple as a ripple effect for wanting to be friends with someone who doesn't reciprocate the feeling or feeling excluded due to labels that society imposes on us. Rejection often leaves us feeling bitter and can even trigger feelings of shame. Unwanted attention, such as overhearing a negative conversation about yourself, can also lead to feeling vulnerable and ashamed. Additionally, failing to achieve a set of goals can be a disappointing and demotivating experience, leaving one feeling like they let themselves down.

I am a woman with many emotions. Just like the ocean, sometimes, it gets rough, or it may be calm. That is nature, which is in our nature as human beings. We do not affirm a rough day on the ocean. Instead, we observe it and learn about the tides, waves, and ripples, which gives us the data to determine when it is a good day to go surfing.

The news of my husband's crime triggered unwelcome emotions, but the underlying burden did not originate from his actions alone. It began with the little girl within me who had learned to conceal herself behind a wall of shame, always seeking to reinforce that wall. Yet, despite her efforts, emotions were integral to who she was and could not be suppressed. She struggled to appreciate the beauty of her emotions and failed to observe them, much like how some people avoid the ocean for fear of drowning.

Growing up in the mountains, I never learned to swim. At the beach, I would only sit at the edge, allowing the gentle ripples to tickle my feet. Similarly, I had avoided fully embracing my emotions and choosing to deal with them.

You do not know if you are not exposed.

I have often asked, "Why me?" on my life's journey, but I never got any definite answer. Now that I have endured many hardships and challenges, I can answer the "why me" question. I realized that the moment my husband robbed a bank, I was still running away from a feeling.

Humans develop habits that we exhibit in patterns laced with feelings. You are either running away from, after, or embracing an outcome. If you are unaware of the chase, then, like me, you will be stuck on a hamster wheel going round and round--again and again in the same cycle.

I was born and raised on the beautiful island of Jamaica in an area called Blue Mountain Peak. It is well known for its unique and authentic Blue Mountain Peak Coffee. As a little girl, I can remember picking coffee with my cousins for my grandmother so she could take it to the local factory. My grandmother was a farmer, and she loved her garden and fields. We raised farm animals like chickens, pigs, goats, and cows. There was never a dull moment at Grandma's house.

I consider myself a small-town girl, a bit shy, but bold enough to tackle a ball. Leaving Jamaica when I was young to come to the United States was life-changing. A small-town girl in a big city can be frightening and intimidating. Landing a job when I entered the States was very rough. It was an increased imposter syndrome for me. Why? It was my first job, and all I could think of daily was, "Is today going to be the day I get fired?"

You do not know because you are not exposed; it is as it is said. You do not know every single person's personal experience or emotions they share. You do not know every solution to a problem. You do not fully understand the capacity of human development. You do not know your limit until you have reached that limit. You do not know until you are exposed. This fundamental approach helps us understand better why we do not pass judgment on each other.

We all have different types and levels of exposure experience. The feeling of being the center of the sirens, notes being taken, eyes looking everywhere, and yellow tape off caution signs granted me the experience of unexpected exposure. The exposure opened up my mental ability, spirituality, and awareness. At that moment, I fought shame, fear, worry, and death.

I cried, pushing me further in the back, hiding me from the exposure. But still, I am going through the process. What do you need next, Mr. Officer? Time stopped for me, but everyone and everything around me was still moving.

Dialogue in my head:

"Wait a minute now, Stephanie, you weren't the one who robbed the bank?"

"No, you are right, I am sure of that, but was it a man down the street or a far-away cousin? No!"

"Where are you, husband?" I thought. "I am so mad at you right now. If you only know how stinking upset I am at you. Why would you do this to us? Please, please, please, I hope you are not dead. Please just come home."

"Are you crazy? He is not coming home." I answered myself. *"Don't you see what he has done? Girl, get your shit together. He is not coming home."*

"Stephanie, you are just as stupid as they come. Why did you choose this life?"

"These officers probably believe I am such an idiot. Look how they look at me; they probably think I am a foolish girl."

"Well, you probably are; who else's husband you know did something this big?"

My emotions were projecting and transcribing, switching from thoughts and feelings to thoughts and sensations.

"Mrs. Harrington, we are still looking for your husband. Do you know where he might have gone to hide?"

"No, Sir."

At that moment, my self-judgment was brutal. You are probably saying, *But it's not your fault!* That is true, but it did not feel like the truth. Taking on the victim role was my comfort zone. This behavior was my norm. It helped me better rationalize the situation and made it easier for me to handle it.

I have an inner voice that can be very harsh and critical. Self-judgment can be especially harmful when it becomes a chronic thinking pattern, leading to negative self-perception and undermining my sense of worth and confidence. After adopting this habit over a long time, I programmed my self-worth by thinking I deserved everything coming to me.

CHAPTER SEVEN:
THE SEARCH

The search for the bandit continued. No one knew where my husband was, not the officer or our family. I was not searching; I was waiting. I could not leave the house even if I wanted to. Is it normal for the officers to stay at your home the entire time? I did not know because this was my first rodeo. But if I went out looking, where would I look? I thought, maybe at his workplace.

That was the only place I knew he went to daily. They say leopards never change their spots.

I approached things the same way in our marriage. I always held on to what he said or did from before. I never looked through a clean slate or a fresh pair of eyes. Or give him the benefit of the doubt. I held on to past arguments and disagreements like I was keeping score. I would remind him of what he said in the last argument and kept repeating it. I was accustomed to repeating what someone did or said before without pardon or letting them off the hook. I learned this growing up and was not aware it was a bad trait that carried into my marriage. This may have been a habit, but it was not good for our relationship.

At the beginning of our marriage, we got a joint bank account, with the expectation that my money is yours and yours is mine. Oh, what a relief to finally have two incomes! This agreement started as a great idea. I got your back, and you got my back kind of a deal. That was our belief until I realized we needed money management. I expected him not to take money out of the account without telling me, and he expected me to do the same. In my mind, I believe I did not have to say anything to him because I was using it to pay the bills and keep us afloat. He believed he did not have to tell me because he is not a child who needed to report to his mother.

The search for meaning and balance began with who has the more convincing narrative to create a non-conflict conversation. Who will the finger be pointed at, and can you justify your answer? This was not a reality in our book; we were two young people, newlyweds with a newborn baby, and we were learning to search for security from each other. In other words, *How far can we go?* We always fought about what was necessary to spend money on but not what was essential. What I believed was of value, and what he believed was not of value. I often thought we should compromise, but even the compromise could be misused.

My background mainly was living from the mindset of lack. I believed in saving and looking for deals or bargains to feel like we won and spent the money correctly. His money philosophy was more along the lines of buying what he wanted when he wanted. Two people with different viewpoints on such an essential matter in a marriage. This was a delicate subject for me because I needed security, and money was a form of security, whether it was a healthy way of thinking or not; at that time of my life, that's all I knew.

It did not take long for us to finally get separate accounts because we did not see eye to eye on the matter. I had seen many marriages and relationships end because of money disagreements. Having a separate account made me feel safe and in control. Having a joint account meant being stretched out of my comfort zone, causing me to micromanage my husband's spending, which came as an attack on his character and trustworthiness. I would try to eliminate any reason for an altercation to keep the peace and hold tight to what I had been fighting for my entire life.

Money can hold various meanings for different people. To some, it represents freedom, while for others, it buys pleasure. Some people, however, view it as an evil force. I wanted to avoid experiencing the vulnerability and stress of falling behind on bills or needing more money when needed. The idea of not being able to pay my bills caused me immense emotional distress. Therefore, I reverted to my old habits and followed the pattern I saw growing up. I asked my husband to give me his portion of the money at the end of the week, and I took care of everything. This approach worked before we married, so I saw no need to change it. He experienced life differently than I did, but he did not fight me; he gave me what I wanted.

I found solace in managing my finances, giving me a sense of control and security. Sharing that responsibility with someone else felt like a risk I was not willing to take. It dawned on me that I could not expect to trust someone else if I did not trust myself first. We should have been united in every aspect of life as a married couple; however, our traditions, beliefs, and finances remained separate, only coming together in some areas, such as our shared bedroom, meals, love, and family time. We committed to becoming one when we married, but we needed to understand what that entailed fully. Despite loving my husband wholeheartedly, I was still deciding whether to entrust anyone with full access to my finances.

It was hit or miss to see eye to eye on money. When my husband and I were newlyweds, I was not wealthy with millions of dollars, but I was a hard worker who understood the worth of each drop of sweat shed to earn every penny. Our perspectives on money differed significantly. He viewed it as a means to achieve desires, while I viewed it as a necessity for survival. Was money the factor causing this difference in beliefs? Of course not; money is tangible currency such as bills, coins, or credit notes. The significance we attach to our personal views on money influences our beliefs.

Have you ever experienced a period in your life when everything seemed uncertain? You felt lost and directionless, and your reality did not align with your plans. You were so deeply immersed in it that even your loved ones could not understand what you were going through. It is a time when you were disconnected, not yet experiencing a midlife crisis, but old enough to be on your own. It is when you must take responsibility for your life, but you may not be ready yet. The internal struggle to determine who would emerge victorious and how long it would take could be challenging.

Sometimes, we silently admit that we are not ready for something, and our behavior reflects it. I was lost and searching for myself, longing for the carefree days of childhood. Yet here I am, married with a family and unprepared for everything. Neither my husband nor I had any training for this, and we were just doing our best with what we had learned based on our past experiences.

It can be a struggle between breaking free from what we experienced as kids and avoiding repeating the same mistakes. But even as adults, we still face some of the same challenges. Everyone is looking for us; there's an invisible expectation to conform to society's norm. It can feel like a collar around our necks is holding us back.

Searching requires asking questions; sometimes, the answers may take time and effort. Even if we already have the answer, we may need to learn its simplicity or how to handle the truth. The truth can seem complex and unfamiliar, and accepting it may require us to change who we are, which can be challenging. I realized I needed to ask the right questions to the right person. That person is self. I believed I did not have the answers from childhood, so why would I even bother asking myself questions?

Questions are made for a reason; I find that because I did not ask a lot of questions, I was not a good problem solver. Instead, I would just take what looked good at face value and run with it, especially if that was what everyone else was doing.

As a young woman from a small town, my access to information and knowledge was limited. When I got married at the age of twenty-six, I believed that I had everything figured out. How wrong I was! I thought I knew how to manage a household and be the ideal wife, but the truth was that I did not. I realized I was stubborn, narrow-minded, afraid of making mistakes, and terrified of rejection.

The concept of a glass being half full or half empty is common, suggesting that we have a choice in how we view things. In my case, my glass was already full, and pouring more into it would have been a waste. I wanted to add more to my life but needed to figure out how to make room for it. I was hesitant to let go of anything, and I struggled to accept the reality that I needed to make changes. I needed to open up more and trust the unknown, but I kept policing and patrolling to keep the peace. But was the peace within the relationship or the peace only in my mind?

It was peaceful in my mind. I believed I had to hold on to control, even though my husband urged me to let go. This mindset prevented me from opening doors to new opportunities for learning, growth, and expansion. For example, I could have considered leaving our joint account to see how things would go in the long run. There were two sides to this decision: on the one hand, I might have been seen as irresponsible or taken advantage of, but on the other hand, I could have been brave enough to allow us to experience not having and learning our lessons through life's experiences. But my mindset was to avoid the pain of lack by getting a separate account.

I realized the importance of focusing on my actions and intentions rather than being fixated on the result. Initially, I intended to provide security and act responsibly. Still, upon reflection, I realized that my decision was primarily motivated by my fear of being stranded in the wilderness for an extended period. Acknowledging this truth was difficult, as it exposed that my mindset was driven entirely by misguided fear. I thought I was saving myself, but it took more time to learn how to fully open my heart to trust.

Admitting this truth required me to acknowledge my mistake, which I had always prided myself on avoiding, as it may have indicated weakness. I recall arguing with my husband, who would say, "You're right, I'm wrong, I'm sorry," which was a foreign concept. Instead, I was accustomed to responding with "You're right, BUT..." always leaving me with the upper hand. At that point in my life, I needed to understand that everyone makes mistakes, and that having flaws and imperfections is normal. I was not aware of this and was still trying to create a picture-perfect life like the ones portrayed in movies and magazines instead of focusing on reality. I was playing dollhouse in the real world.

It was more about emulating the ideal without needing to verbalize it and being excessively hard on myself for not achieving what I perceived as the standard. I was constantly judging myself, and everything seemed to impede my progress. I held myself to such a high standard, one I could not reach, passing harsh judgment on myself with no leniency.

This self-judgment served as a gateway to the judgment of others, as I was more forgiving and understanding of others than I was of myself. Practicing self-compassion and showing kindness and understanding instead of harsh judgment was crucial. Unfortunately, I was not aware of this and could not show myself compassion even if I wanted to. I had learned to show compassion towards others but never towards myself, always being overly critical in any given situation.

How I talked to myself was far from how I would speak to others. I was my harshest critic, and nobody could bring me down more than I could. I subjected myself to unwarranted judgment based on limited information about life.

CHAPTER EIGHT:
SELF-LOVE IS THE FIRST LOVE

Finally, the officers gave me my phone. They still do not know my husband's whereabouts. What now? I thought. The officers were getting ready to leave, and so was I. I got my daughter, and off we went to my father's home. Looking back in the mirror at my daughter sitting calmly and playing with her toys saddened my heart. I felt the pressure of not giving her what I did not have.

We drove silently to my destination. I pulled into the driveway and took the baby out of the car. I was very hesitant to go inside the house. My imagination started running wild with the burden of unloading what was happening to my family. I slowly opened the door and walked into the house as if nothing had happened. My dad was home, and by the look of things, it looked like he had not seen the news yet. I did not know how to give him the news. So, I sat around the table, looking puzzled and lost. I guess I wanted him to say something first.

Then I said quietly, "You will not believe what happened."

With his head down, facing the bowl on the table because he was eating, he shook his head, which meant for me to tell him what happened, and there it was. I told him, and then the crying started again. My dad kept silent for a minute as if he were collecting his thoughts or did not know what to say.

n my culture, parents are not the ones to engage in conversation; they prefer to preach. The silence from my dad was to get his message together.

My dad went off on one of his sermons, and I became the congregation. I felt like I was standing in the middle of a dartboard, with projectiles approaching me from every direction, but none hitting the bull's eye. You would have thought I was the one who committed the crime. I thought he probably did not know how to handle a situation like this or he was in shock, but neither did I. I desperately needed a comforting voice. Instead, my dad's sermon turned into a comedy show, and he started laughing. It was a strange and shocking response, which left me feeling bewildered.

You might wonder why my dad would laugh in such a heartbreaking time. Maybe it was a sign of a defense mechanism. At a time when my life was falling apart, I felt like the people I had trusted were mocking me. But behind that laughter, I believed it was all the thoughts going through his mind. The traffic in his mind was congested; the unexpected news caused a bumper-to-bumper traffic jam without knowing how the journey would end. Not only was there a traffic jam, but people were looking at what caused it, which made him very uncomfortable because it was connected to him through me.

While still in the middle of digesting the news about my husband's bank robbery and getting a sermon preached to me, my dad exited the table and began marching towards the front door, muttering and talking. He even switched lanes and brought up my marriage as a lesson from God. I felt trapped in the chair I was sitting in, unable to escape the judgmental words. The entire evening was centered around how I had supposedly brought shame and disgrace to the family and how people would perceive us. From where I was sitting, I could not understand how marrying the person I loved and starting a wonderful family was something to be ashamed of. If that was my "crime," I was ready to serve my time.

At that moment, I was told to divorce my husband immediately. I was told he was no good for me, that he had ruined my life and brought me disgrace. According to my dad, "The devil sent him to destroy you," and "Your child is a descendant of the devil." When I said that darts were coming at me, I was not exaggerating.

Self-love was not a common practice for me. I used to believe the stigma of self-love being selfish, egotistical, or having a narcissistic taste to it. I struggled with self-love; some of the reasons are growing up without enough self-acceptance, too much shame, and my trust in others being shattered. Turning my attention to myself taught me that self-love is about embracing all aspects of myself, including my strengths and weaknesses. Accepting myself entirely seemed strange because of my self-judgments. I had to learn to be selfish with my attention and make the extra effort to learn about my thought patterns, mood swings, emotions, and behaviors.

I would do my reflections daily and ask myself these three questions:

1.   How was the traffic today?
2.   What did you learn today?
3.   What are you grateful for today?

These three simple questions can do wonders if you practice them daily. To explain what I mean by traffic . . . thoughts flood our minds all day. I want you to think about the highway with all the cars switching lanes, some speeding, accidents, road rage, and so much more happening on the road. Answering the questions give you feedback on how you handled the traffic for that day regarding your thoughts. The thoughts will come, but how did you react? Did you switch lanes or stop on the side of the road . . . meaning did you stay stuck on a thought that took over your entire day? Did you get upset and flick someone off? Did you poke your head out the window and scream at the person who cut you off? Did you feel overwhelmed, and if so, what was the trigger? If it came around again, could you identify the pattern? And do you have a plan to deal with that traffic signal?

The world is a big classroom; we are always learning something. If you missed a lesson because you did not reflect on the day or even be aware, you were placed in a position to grow and become better than the day before. If you missed it, that's okay; life always reintroduces the same lesson again and again until you get it. It is essential to take the time to get to know yourself better. Practicing self-evaluation gives you something to look forward to. Gratitude is a good exercise to help you focus on the good things in your life, creating a good feeling.

It felt like the entire world was against me, like I was backed into a corner, and everyone said, "Gotcha!" It is not about what you do when everyone is watching but what you do when standing alone for something you believe in. And the people you expect to support you and have your back tell you to let go, give up, and walk away. It felt like a million different voices were screaming in my head. But it did not feel like I had the decision to make; I knew I had already made a decision when I said, "I do." I chose to marry the man I loved, for better or worse. I was facing the worst. My experiences have taught me the importance of questioning and examining my words, beliefs, and values and not blindly following what others tell me.

Breaking away from this mentality can be challenging, particularly when it has been deeply ingrained in your life, and you have been conditioned to believe that you must adhere to a narrative that appears reasonable to you, especially if it is connected to God. The mere mention of the name God is both a symbol of liberation and a tool for oppression. I have lived several years believing that my misfortunes were divine retribution, even though I could not explain for what precisely. Nonetheless, I was convinced of the narrative.

When you are raised in a home that labels you as God's child or the devil, and you have an understanding of the devil that means you are not good, not compliant, or possibly having some kind of demon or spirit inside you, all you want is not to be associated with such a label. That is the curse word for Christians--a word I heard more in my home than the word love. Do not get me wrong, I, too, fell prey to words and their tone and projection of my ideas on others. I used to look past being human and thought I was so spiritual that I had the right to dictate what I believed to be accurate. From my experience, it is a vain and ignorant sense of entitlement to feel special without understanding the consequences or the energy passed down to others. As a mother, it was heartbreaking to see how an innocent child can suffer from a family's misguided judgment.

Despite being surrounded by criticism from various directions, I remained steadfast in my beliefs and held on tightly to the values of love, grace, and building relationships. I never accepted what others told me at face value; instead, I always tried to get to know people and make my own decisions based on that understanding.

It is natural to want to go along with the crowd and adopt their beliefs when, around you, everyone is doing it, but it takes courage to stand up for what you believe in, particularly when it clashes with those closest to you. I was aware of the bond I had with my husband, but I also recognized that what my family views as their truth is their reality, and there is little I can do to alter their perspective. However, I can follow my heart rather than my eyes.

I was in a mental battle as night fell, contemplating every possible scenario, outcome, what-if, and hope. Everyone else had retired to bed, but sleep eluded me. My mind was consumed with whether my husband was lurking near the house and, if so, what might happen if he showed up. I was afraid to shut my eyes, praying that he was alive and that the situation would resolve without harming anyone.

Despite barely sleeping and only managing to close my eyes for around thirty minutes, I forced myself to get up, get dressed, and head off to school. The next day was a day of testing, and as usual, I knew I had to be strong and face whatever challenges lay ahead.

When I arrived at the hospital where I was doing my internship, I sat in my car, gathering all the strength I could muster to face my colleagues in the department. I hesitated to go in but was determined to complete my internship program. As I walked through the front door, all eyes were on me, and there was a palpable awkwardness. They did not know what to say, and I was not offering any information.

I held my head high, my eyes forward, and simply said, "Good morning," as I completed my morning equipment quality control. Despite feeling like time was moving in slow motion, I managed to push through my fears and take my test before preparing to leave for the day.

In this situation, I felt entirely out of my depth. I had no answers, no idea what would happen next, and no clue what my future would hold. All I knew was that I was afraid, scared, angry, and desperately calling for help.

In my moment of distress, I realized quickly that I had no choice but to face what circumstances had chosen me. It was a path I never envisioned for myself and no one in my circle of influence had ever experienced. I was left with the option to move forward into the unknown or listen to those who claimed to know what they would do if they were in my shoes. The following day after the bank robbery was even worse. Time seemed to amplify my pain and stretch out my longing. Time is constant, moving forward and remaining indifferent no matter how much I cried, wished, and hoped. Time was created to serve me, but I was doing everything possible to stop it. At the present moment, they have forced me to confront my situation.

At a particular time of the day, the news repeats itself, and breaking news like a bank robbery is sure to be on replay. I was standing in the hospital coffee shop, getting something to drink; at the corner of my eye, pictures of my baby girl and I were on the screen, along with my husband's. The headline read, "The search for the Dapper Bandit continues; he is armed and dangerous." My head was down, my chest tightened, and I began to breathe very heavily. It seemed like any other day for people in the coffee shop, but I was devastated.

This situation was causing me to experience feelings I wanted to avoid at all costs, a price I was not willing to pay voluntarily. I would have chosen a different scene and storyline if it were up to me.

My whole demeanor was to avoid confrontation with anyone. People like to ask questions, and so do I. The question may not be directly communicated, but through one's eye, it is. I did not understand that I was the one adding extra fuel to my fire, a prominent blind spot I had ignored for years. I was too harsh and unkind to myself. In my quest to uncover the many layers of the belief in shame, I found that the way one views the world or people is how they view themselves and their situation. My conditioning towards judging people was very critical and demanding. I was the keeper of "you should," a very naughty truth to admit but the truth that set me free.

Sometimes, we hold on to the very thing that holds us back, and it is never always a person. It may be a belief. I was fighting more with a belief of unwanted exposure and going against social norms than the act of the bank robbery itself.

CHAPTER NINE:
THE UNDOING

Unwrapping the layers of low-energy thinking, beliefs, and emotions is a thin line to tread. Only some people are willing to be honest with themselves; being honest is more challenging than you think. I entertained the many reasons to continue with the two opponents' approach. My conditioning exposed me to consistently having two characters at all times in the center of my stage. One character is to blame, and the other character I should wait on.

These characters have their brand personalities and names. Some names are widely known, so when mentioned, everyone knows what they stand for. I have lived between these two opponents for many years; one, I believed, fought against me, and the other fought for me. I had never met any of the opponents physically before at that time in my life, but the narrative I carried created the belief I chose to carry on throughout my journey.

The villain and the hero, the good versus the evil. This joint approach is adopted in many industries, mainly to capitalize on the movie industry, the media, religion, culture, race, etc. I was always captivated by the hero or good character. I invested my mental capital into whatever the character inspired. I wanted so badly to be identified with the hero's character.

Over the years, my mental skills to be the hero became stronger and stronger, just like going to the gym and building physical muscle. The more my belief was inspired, the stronger my mental muscle grew and the more attracted I was to a character. Not only was I inspired by the character I identified with, but I was even more motivated to determine the character of the people around me. My mental muscle was way more developed to look for a character in others than to look for the character in myself.

The essential tool for developing my mental muscle is belief. Most of the time, I train my mind without evidence or fact, which is acceptable because the mental landscape is invisible. Misusing this tool can create space for mind control. With that being said, according to the ancient text, I would like to use the statement "like sheep to the slaughter." This tool also caused me to invest in someone else's life narrative.

As mentioned in previous chapters, I colored outside the lines as a little girl. I did not like the image of myself in my head because it did not look like the social norm. That was the beginning of the dual character approach in my life. One character says color outside the lines; the other says, no, hide your drawing; no one wants to see that; they will talk about you. As I grew older, my environment helped me build the strength of each character trait.

The only difference between when I was much younger and when I got older was that I did not give my characters names like Good and Evil. That is something I learned from my environment. I grew up enforcing the character approach and using this approach to label people based on their actions. The twist for me was when I demonstrated the exact actions for which I judged others but felt as though I was justified in doing whatever I did. Because I believed I was the only one who knew what I had gone through and how it felt.

With time by my side, I realized no one was coming to help me with my mismark. For example, time made me realize my parents were the Santa Claus. Becoming a mother made me the tooth fairy. These ideas, however, are a great way to ignite the imagination in the minds of children. But being an adult, I was still waiting for my hero. I was still waiting for someone to save me. I had a life filled with hardship and pain I was holding on to them even though I claimed to have let go of it all.

I waited and waited and waited some more, and it took a long time for me to realize no one was coming. So, I did the hardest thing I ever had to endure mentally, and that was to challenge my beliefs and try to understand myself. To "know thyself" is to understand myself. This approach opened up a more profound awareness of the capability of my internal landscape. Then, it became clear that I was simultaneously the hero and the villain. The fight was within me. It was I who embodied both character opponents. But most surprisingly, neither of the characters was right or wrong. Both are simply expressions fueled by my beliefs. An expression I am free to choose each day.

Fear of being on the wrong side and vain thinking led me to believe life was happening to me. Was I the one who enforced meaning to my thoughts and beliefs and created my perceptions? I then knew what to do next: become the change agent and decide to redesign, remodel, and reinvent myself. I chose to learn about myself rather than someone else's narrative of who I am. To be oneself inspires excellent freedom—ability to embrace what I am living and *not* what I lived (which is "devil" spell backwards—did you know?) What was most overbearing for me was the idea that I was being judged by people who shared the same belief and were committed to that belief. First, it took a while to understand why I was so hard on myself due to how I judged others. I had to learn to forgive myself for not knowing what I did not know.

A belief that starts early is deeply rooted and more challenging to uproot. This was very difficult for me. The most comfortable thing to do is to continue believing it is no longer serving me. I wanted something different but did not know how to do it differently. I felt powerless and, at the same time, empowered to wait. My power was deactivated as a child. My mind is my most precious possession, but it was not thinking my thoughts or creating the reality I needed but rather what I thought I should want.

To create a new reality, I had to take the uncomfortable path of being honest with myself, stepping away from a vain mindset, and asking myself the hard questions. Did you deceive yourself? Yes, I did. I am the key to unlocking all doors within me. Perception creates pathways through those doors. Perception is a storyteller that can be deceptive or honest.

Having a victim mindset was not an optimistic or proactive viewpoint for me. My outlook tends to attract more of a poor me pity party. I felt life was hard for everyone but even more challenging for me, and I thought no one understood my pressure. I was good at presenting whatever I was experiencing as the art of someone else's doing. The mirror of my mind was not fully developed, reflecting limited data and understanding. All my life, I looked outside myself to blame and for answers. My mind was trained to create systems for external explanation, which became the default program setting under which I operated.

Breaking that cycle without any awareness is nearly impossible. Looking through a broken lens reflects brokenness, and looking through a happy lens reflects happiness. Looking through a victim lens reflects victimhood. Looking through a powerlessness lens reflects powerlessness. This cycle will continue throughout my journey only until I am ready to face the truth.

A cycle is an interval in which recurring patterns produce the same result. We all go through cycles in our individual lives. Patterns and cycles can be advantageous or disadvantageous depending on the need and productivity of what a person may feel they need or just something they may want to break.

Do you ever have a moment when you say, "I will never do that again," but shortly after, you do what you said you would not do again? At that moment when you confessed not wanting to repeat the same action, you truly meant it. You sincerely mean it when you say it; however, doing it again feels like a betrayal to yourself and possibly someone else, digging you deeper into despair. Belief kills, and belief builds. Before the incident, I wore the victim role of a fighter, a determined woman trying to hold down a family. After the robbery, I wore the victim role of shame, hiding behind my emotional pain.

The Process

We've all heard the age-old advice to "go through the process" and not try to escape it. But let me tell you, it is easier said than done. As someone who has been there, I know firsthand how tempting it is to take shortcuts and skip the hard work. I used to rush through my school assignments to get good grades without understanding the material. And while I might have felt a temporary sense of accomplishment, I was just avoiding the work that would have helped me grow and learn. Looking back, I realize that I was just chasing a feeling. I craved the excitement of finishing something and being praised for it. But in doing so, I was betraying myself. I needed to be more accurate about myself and my potential to learn and grow. I was just seeking attention, desperate for someone to notice me and tell me I was doing a good job.

And I know I am not alone in this. So many of us are taught from a young age that we need to be perfect and that we need to achieve certain things to be valuable. But here's the thing: I did not have to keep living that way. I could embrace the process and dive into the hard work and the challenges that came my way. As I mentioned, you do not know what you do not know. And sometimes, you only have access to information available to you. We are led to believe that some challenges are an attack. I remember saying to myself as a little girl how the wicked sent things to destroy me, without any evidence of this, just by believing a statement that fits right in with the assumed victim role. Therefore, I played defense all my life, fighting an invisible culprit I had never met but whom I blamed for every misfortune or anything that did not go my way.

I would use the common phrase, "I'm still a work in progress," so I do not judge my attitude without being aware that progress is impossible without being optimistic about challenges. If you are not self-aware of taking risks, being creative, and thinking outside the box, you will keep repeating the same cycle, believing that what you know is enough. Awareness that I am the source and solution changed the game of my new approach to "The Process."

If you have ever applied a relaxer or perm to your hair, you know it involves waiting for the chemicals to take effect. I understood the purpose of the relaxer process and did not fight it because we wanted our hair to look good.

When it came to the process of life, however, I struggled to understand its purpose. The victim's mind rejects any idea of the process. Instead of serving my time, I fought for survival, not trying to understand what was real and an illusion. I lived in the world of illusion in my head, creating unrealistic expectations for myself and ultimately becoming delusional. Looking back, I see myself as a chess piece being moved around, with little control over my life.

I had to learn to appreciate the journey, even when it was difficult or uncomfortable. This approach helps me see myself for who I truly am rather than who I've been told to be. I was told I was oppressed; instead of continuing to affirm this label on myself, I gave myself a clearer understanding to not limit my beliefs because of someone else's righteousness. I better understood that I believed in the narrative by affirming the labels as my own and identifying with them by defending myself.

It all depends on the lens you look through and your perception of life. This was my experience and my approach. I became my own worst enemy, a carrier of an illusion based on a narrative that looks real and sounds good. This journey was a process in itself for me. Honestly, at first, it was a hard pill to swallow, and I needed someone or something to blame, especially when I felt like I missed out on a lot in life.

My questions kept surfacing, and I wanted justification. Accepting that I played a significant part in mental conditioning was difficult because I believed I was innocent of the motives behind the purpose. Therefore, I did not stop there; I decided to go deeper. To look through the lens of the benefit of the doubt.

The ego wanted revenge, and I was again in the middle of another fight. They misled me; they were the culprit, whoever they were. My grandmother would say, "Jump out of the fire and into the frying pan." I had to contend with my mind that NOW I am the conscious creator in my life. I can choose what I want to grow in my mind and ultimately manifest in our world.

I chose the narrative I want to live by, not my pain, unforgiveness, or ego. This is Now my story. I am that girl who never gave up on herself. I went through the fire as gold and came out gold. The fire burned away all the impurities and gave me a lifetime of experience that I can now use to help others choose better, not bitter.

I did not know the purpose of the process, but if there was one thing the process taught me, it was "who I am." So do not be afraid to go through the process; take time to understand it. It might be challenging, but it is worth it in the end.

Nightfall came, and it was about time for the evening news. I got a call that my husband had been found. Just like that, life created another shift in our family lives. The question remains: Is this the beginning or the end? Is the beginning of a new journey or the end of the old? Regardless of the direction, I was not up for the challenge. I did not ask many questions; honestly, I did not know what to say. I did not know what the future held; experiencing the unknown was unfamiliar territory, even at the hand of faith.

CHAPTER TEN:
"WHY" DO WE JUDGE OURSELVES?

There are many reasons why people might judge themselves. Some common factors are setting high standards; people who set high standards for themselves may feel they need to meet them. Past experiences, such as negative feedback or criticism from others, can lead to feelings of self-doubt and insecurity that can contribute to self-judgment. Social norms of "you should" hold us captives of societal expectations or criteria. I am guilty, charged, and sentenced to years, afraid of being myself or even trying to know myself because of the pressure to conform to specific standards of success or appearance.

The common denominator in all scenarios is ourselves. We judge others because we first judge ourselves. We were not born critical; we learn how to adapt the trait. The more we become critical of ourselves and others, the more it feels normal until it becomes ingrained in us and ultimately gets passed down through generations. We consider ourselves according to what we believe and think and what our environment taught us based on someone else's experience. Understanding that we are observers helps create a better perspective in seeing rather than adapting.

Assessing ourselves is a good thing; it is one of the vital awareness elements. Suppose we begin to practice asking ourselves why we criticize ourselves and others. We would be surprised that most answers are because of "you should" past programming. You should *look* like, you should *be* like, and you should *do it* like. When your life does not *look* like it, you should *be* like it and *do it* like *it*. You judge yourself and others for not believing in "you should."

I realized that I needed to analyze two sides when judging myself. This approach influences open-mindedness. Throughout my journey, I played the judge and prosecutor role but not so much the lawyer. My judgment was harsh and heavy. The reason why I beat myself up so much is that I believed I should have known better. My accepted belief in that narrative helped shape my internal self-image. My self-image was mainly negative because I was not meeting the standard I set so high for myself. And I could not help but add all the negative criticism I learned from hearing others talk about other people.

I needed a good defense lawyer to defend me regardless of the charge. But I was not that good to myself because I did not know what I did not know. I believed the guilt laid upon me by another's action forced responsibility. I convinced myself I should have known better when life is about adventure, curiosity, and freedom to explore. Our internal instinct does not comply with man-made rules and conditioning. But if we believe we do, then that belief is what is accepted in our mind.

Having a good defense lawyer means defending my well-being and being purposeful in my existence and the life I am now living. This approach is significantly complex when your environment influences and labels you to live a certain way. A defense lawyer's argument must be louder and more convincing than the prosecutor's. A defense lawyer helps you right your wrongs.

A defense lawyer would represent positive self-talk. A voice that argues and defends my freedom. This voice was not developed as a child, at least not for me. I did not know how to fight for myself mentally. I was taught to fight an external entity that I had never met, but I created a mental image from the narrative told to me. That image grew bigger and bigger, taking up more territory in my mind daily.

The more I felt terrible about myself, the more I blamed the eternal entity for making me feel that way; now, we have become rivals, and the court battle begins. This battle is only accepted because I choose to believe it. I am the only way to my mind and my heart. That was the penalty for being a child without awareness or understanding of mental capital. But then, a lawyer could argue that it is not the responsibility of the environment to help mold a child's mind. Yes, I agree that it is the parents' responsibility, but the sad thing is that they are also under the same mind control.

I even got creative when I learned I could name each entity. As a little girl, I remember the first time I paid attention to the name the Devil. He sounded scary and evil, and immediately, I was afraid of him. I had never seen him, but I understood it was because he was a spirit. I had never seen a spirit before, good or bad, but I believed it was true. This information allowed me to choose which entity to blame for my life's good and evil.

From my experience, the two names, God and the Devil, were not just a religion. It was a weapon of war and the perception of a peacemaker. People would label you or themselves based on their opinion of which entity or rule they believe you belong to. This is all regarding how you made them feel or due to their self-righteousness if you abide by the "you should" societal norm or their biblical definition or translation.

Growing up attending Sunday school, I would listen to the stories and try to imagine each character. You better believe I did not want anything to do with an evil character. I wanted to be the good girl, the obedient child, and I tried everything possible to become that girl. Everyone wants to be a good person. No one wants to be seen as wrong or labeled evil. With my new approach to life, I decided not to read into the bible but out of it. What do I mean by this? Reading into the bible means I would read the bible the same way the story was told. I opened no room for questioning because that would feel like a betrayal to God. Reading out of the bible is reading the text without preconceptions and meaning.

I witnessed a lot of "love with conditions" growing up. Even I adapted this trait. This meant that you would get praise and acceptance because you did something to make the other person feel good. You would get the opposite if you made someone feel bad. It is crazy that the dysfunction of one person's feelings rests upon another person for them to control. It shocked me when I met my husband and his family; their cultural norm somewhat displayed unconditional love. They had a good lawyer who looked behind the charge and saw the person. Yes, they still felt the guilt and may have had to spend some time in "upset" jail, but at the core, they understood that they are loved.

That was not my case; I did not know how to defend my heart and pardon my ignorance from myself. All conditioning starts somewhere. The lawyer I had I was told was Jesus, but from my understanding, I would not have to do anything; He would take care of everything. So, I could continue with my mess, and He would clean it up; by the way, there is no need to learn how to defend myself; just accept being a victim and wait for His return. Everyone's perceptions and beliefs are different. I am sure others from my environment grew up with opinions different from my experience. To be clear, I am talking about the court appearance in our mind; some call it the battleground.

Think of your mind as a courthouse. You are faced with a situation and must decide how to solve the problem. Who shows up, the prosecutor presenting the problem, the lawyer defending the problem, and the judge deciding the verdict. The jury helps make the decisions, comprising everything you learned and experienced, your beliefs and perceptions, background, cultural differences, and biases from the day you were born.

Now, in my courtroom, the judge is the people I admire, my beliefs about their opinions. Respect and honor carry weight in their words and expectations. I can sum this up by saying "what they believed." I was always concerned with what others thought about me. This mindset created an uncompassionate judge who laid down their laws.

The prosecutor is all the things they would disapprove of. I would make my case with a compelling story based on their approval, created by my perception. Sometimes, they speak loudly or very softly but make their presence known.

My defender comprises my experiences of seeing others defend themselves or fall prey to the cultural norm. How loud were they? Were they making noise or keeping quiet? It all depends on the person's perception. But in my psychological courtroom, I was driven by fear; I did not want to comply but felt I had to, especially if I wanted to be right with God based on my belief at that time.

From my experience, there are better ways to live. This path took me down the road of wearing a mask. Masks are superficial and can be used to cover up or hide behind an egotistical front. Webster's dictionary defines a mask as: "worn as a disguise, to amuse or terrify other people." Wearing different masks was my norm, and I was comfortable living my lie, but I was not tricking anyone but myself. I wore a mask of fake humility to cover up my hurt and shame, pretending to be okay but feeling empty inside.

The deception was that I could wear fake humility while looking firm with a smile and a friendly handshake. I never wanted to be considered vulnerable because that would make me look weak. The only person who knew what was happening inside me was me.

But it could hurt the case when you do not have a strong and experienced lawyer.

My lawyer is my mindset, my authentic self's most accurate version of me. My lawyer only sometimes shows up for court, and there are many different reasons. For one, she may be covered under too many labels, have different arguments to consider, try to figure out details, or not believe in herself enough. One of the main reasons my lawyer was not showing up was that she had limited information about the case; she only had what was available.

Some trials take longer than others. It all depends on the evidence and persuasive statements. Enough information allows you to present opinions and decide what's best for your world. What trials have you been through in your life? How long did it take, or is it still happening? Is your authentic self showing up in court, or is it the one behind the mask?

I wondered if other people had the same thoughts as I did. But no two people are the same, even with similar experiences. It got to the point wherein I just got sick and tired of being sick and tired. The best way I can explain it is that I was at the end of my movie. I was tired of being in an insanity mode of doing the same thing repeatedly and expecting different results.

It was like I did not care anymore--trying to control everything. You could say I just let go! Letting go for me was the hardest thing because fear was the soul tie, the connecting bond between my true self and who I pretended to be. When I say I pretended to be someone else, I was not aware of my pretending; therefore, it was not pretending to be me. It was who I believed I was.

I believed I was a mistake, a troublemaker, and a disruptor, and sometimes, I believed I was the police holding the lawbreakers accountable for breaking the rules. What I figured out, though, was that I had to break the rules and think outside the cage around my mind to find my true self. Breaking an internal belief is challenging. The cognitive dissonance is brutal, but sometimes, that's what it takes to win the case.

Because I judge myself so badly, it makes me judge others the same. I would use my Judge, prosecutor, lawyer, and jury mindset to judge another person's case. But the reality is they did not hold my judge's opinions high, and they did not learn and experience life the same way I did, and their lawyer may show up for them differently.

You see this more often in marriages and intimate relationships. In my marriage, my judgment tried all the cases. My husband's judgment was not relevant to me at the early stage of our marriage because I was still operating my office with limited information and experience. I was not exposed enough to other opinions; I was just used to one way of thinking.

If you are married or in any relationship, you may recall disagreeing with your spouse or partner, friend, etc., and believing your judgment is always right. No, think about this: why do you believe you were right? Was it because you have a belief that justifies your opinion? Is it because your viewpoint is considered normal or more common? Do both of you value the same opinion? The more people are on board with a particular belief, the more convincing it is.

Did I mention my husband is Italian, and I am Jamaican? When we got married, we had different mindsets, opinions, ideas, and ways of living, but one thing we had in common was the courtroom. Love is our courtroom where all the cases are held. Whether the lawyers, the judge, or the jury showed up, our love was always there and waiting to facilitate any argument. Love's Courtroom gave us enough space and time to work out our case and develop a better verdict. Even though we have the space and time, the challenge lies in letting go of what we hold dearly individually to experience something different; it is like stepping into the unknown, not knowing how it will work out, but you are willing to let go of your opinions of right and wrong.

With ourselves, we decide who is right and wrong based on our judge's influences. But in our love courtroom, his and my opinions matter, not my friends, pastor, mother, father, principal, doctor, influencers, politicians, etc.

In the love courtroom, we practice silencing the voices and embracing the two, becoming one.

Do not get it twisted; it did not happen overnight. We were thrown into a courtroom without experience or enough information; all we had was each other and our baggage. Sometimes, I showed up to court alone, and sometimes, he showed up to court alone; then, there were times when none of us showed up.

While we presented evidence and compelling arguments, our lawyers were behind the scenes, trying to determine ways to win the case. Most of the time, one of us had to cave and give in on the verdict. We had about the same number of charges stacked against us. Even though he was from the streets and I was from the jungle, he had his own deep-rooted beliefs, and I had my own deep-rooted beliefs that we both had to work on within ourselves.

A good lawyer will tell you never to take the stand. Leave that up to the witnesses. Witnesses share their experiences with you and their views towards the case. Most of our witnesses were close family members on both sides. When they take the stand, they present their traditions and cultures and provide evidence to protect their bloodline.

The lawyers have a way of reiterating to the jury that our character is not on trial but which crime we committed. Is it a crime to set boundaries with self and others? Is it a crime to let go of cultural norms? Is it a crime to live the life you wanted? Is it a crime not to know the root of our emotional pain? Is it a crime to avoid getting our expectations met? Is it a crime to be immature? Is it a crime to love one another?

Consistently, we had to attend court, listening to all our past programming make their case. I, for one, can remember taking the stand at every court appearance, pleading my case to the jury, and sharing my viewpoint as justified; after all, mine was considered righteous. There was no taking responsibility on my end. I will likely leave it up to the lawyers to defend me. The court was only sometimes a happy place. It takes too much energy, and you hear things you forgot about years before and then have to face it again.

Taking the case up in your hand permits you to meet your authentic self, your most faithful version on the stand. He or she will fight to the death for you, even if it means going deeper within, being completely honest with yourself, and facing the reality of choosing to be happy or right. This is a choice only the most authentic version of you can make because it requires courage.

Courage to stand alone, go against your ego, and be vulnerable, to let your guard down and open your mind to new possibilities, to be willing to try something different that may seem reckless before, but now you are challenging that belief. Or you could choose to remain under the influence of your past judges and build a solid case for them while your relationship sinks.

Noah built his ark to protect himself and his family from the flood, or he could have lived in what everyone else was living. Noah understood the importance of the law of duality; everything happens in the opposite. A male and a female. Your way and my way. Our opinion or their opinion. What is considered suitable, and what is considered wrong? When the flood comes, the argument, the disappointments, the hurt, the blame, the emotional suffering, the political rallies, the government shutdown, the loss of security, and the lies expose what he had built to sustain his new life.

He dared to go deep within, listen to his most authentic self, and build an ark that protected his family. His ark was his love courtroom. He had the same judges, prosecutor, and jury and was faced with limited information about the flood. But he was willing to go where most of us stop, and that is where we accept what they told us our lives should look, feel, and be like. Mass media marketing advertises the perfect life with no flood coming and laughing at you.

Noah was the doer in building his ark, not the actor of someone else's script. He built it himself. My husband and I built our marriage based on our rules, not the opinions of others. Or what we believe others may think about us. It is not a one-person that is building a case of a lifetime. While Noah was building, his wife gathered the animals and put the pieces together. To start their new life after the flood. She saw his vision and was on board with the ark.

I, too, was putting the pieces back together in my mental and emotional intelligence. As a woman, I am, by nature, a life-giver. A portal to this world? I play the same role in the love courtroom. I can give life to myself or damnation. My husband, too, is a life-giver without him. I could not be a portal to this world, but he, too, has to choose to give life to himself or damnation.

It is more challenging when only one person is building and the other is watching or criticizing. I find myself on both sides. I was once the one criticizing while he was building, and then there was a time when I was building while he was criticizing. Sometimes, we are left to figure out ourselves. That is why space and time are needed to support the journey. There is a lot that comes with the architectural work of marriage.

CHAPTER ELEVEN:
THE UNQUENCHED MARRIAGE THIRST

BUILD. GROW. SHINE.

The sun's heat was calming down, and the midafternoon shades were beginning to set. When you need a distraction in a moment of panic, the best thing to do is drink plenty of water. It is the same in marriage when it is under fire. You must find the information and wisdom—the water—to help you survive, to quench the thirst.

When building, you need tools; you cannot build a house without tools. You also need building materials such as wood, plastic, glass, metal, cement, brick, blocks, etc. In most cases, you need a blueprint to lay out the vision to the builder. In Jamaica, up in the mountains, some people build their houses, room by room, with no architectural plan. Eventually, it comes together in the end, but this is due to financial availability.

They usually build a room first to have somewhere to sleep and lay their heads at night when it gets dark and cold. It is the same at the beginning of a marriage; you want someone so you can tell them what's in your head and feel comfortable opening up with them when your mind is at rest. It is easier to sleep well. It makes you feel at ease, like someone has your back while you sleep.

In Jamaica, we have used something called pit toilets. A pit toilet is when you dig a hole and build a wooden seat; no water is connected, just covered with a board when finished. It was always outside, so it was more challenging to get up in the middle of the night to go outside in the dark to use the toilet. Adding a bathroom to the room is the next addition to the house. It is the same in our marriage; we want to be able to let our feces (shit) out in the home, not outside, for everyone would know that we are going to the restroom. I, too, carried this behavior into my marriage and told all the shit that happened between us to others. I acted like I was still using the pit toilet outside in the dark.

Some may add the kitchen next or another room to the house. When food is cooked inside the kitchen, you can smell the aroma in the oven and feel the heat from the pot on the stove. A lot goes into cooking; it takes some experience with seasoning, measuring, and mixing all different ingredients to end up with something delicious. Why am I sharing this? Because it is the same when building yourself or a marriage.

Marriages mirror different ingredients that are mixed to create something extraordinary. The mixing of different opinions, the seasoning of social influences, and measuring comparisons between others. These ingredients all make up a fantastic meal or a not-so-good meal. Nevertheless, these ingredients are tools that help you when cooking. The beauty in cooking is that you can add and take things out, or even reinvent a new recipe. It all depends on what you both can stomach. It is said, "A way to a man's heart is through the stomach." What was I feeding my husband? Was it something delicious or distasteful?

You cannot build a marriage without tools like understanding, open-mindedness, nonjudgment, kindness, and support. Over the years, I have learned that knowing and sharing these things with others is not enough if you are not practicing these characteristics yourself first. Giving yourself the gift of these tools allows you to work on yourself first and become a foundation within the relationship that you can build upon. It is better than showing someone else how to use the tools when you have no experience using them.

Can you imagine telling your husband how to use a wrench when you have never touched one before--only what you saw others do or in a movie? Or telling him how to love you when you do not love yourself? Telling him what you think you want when you do not know what you want but rather what you were conditioned to believe you want?

Very early on in our marriage court, I wanted to be right; he wanted to be happy. He would accept what I deemed wrong, and his apology would sound like, "You know what? You are right; I am sorry." My response would be, "I am tired of you being sorry. You cannot just say you're sorry every time; something must change." There are two things I want to point out here:

1. First, he knew he did not know everything, which allowed him to say, "Sorry." On the other hand, I thought I knew everything, and my ego was so big that saying sorry would mean I was wrong. Growing up, my environment did not practice this behavior. We always said, "The devil is a liar," and continued with the toxic behavior.

2. Secondly, I want to point out that when I told him, "Something must change," I wanted *him* to change. Because my toxic thinking was if *he* changed, everything would be okay. I never thought it was me; I was perfect, but I was in for a rude awakening. I learned very late that if something is outside of your control, i.e., a person, a boss, or a

teacher, the better question is, *how can I learn to let it go?* This is not as easy as it sounds. Just saying I let something go does not mean I did the inner mental work of letting it go. If it were someone I met that I have no attachment to, then yes, I could walk away with no lingering thoughts. But it is not the same when it is someone you love and care for.

It is crazy how we view life circumstances; you would think it should be the opposite. This may not be for everyone; as I mentioned, we all grew up in different environments, and our deep-rooted beliefs are planted differently. One of my toxic behaviors was craving other people's approval. I would never admit this, but deep down, it is the place from which I was operating. Without awareness, I was stuck on this hamster wheel, bleeding energy and attention to feel good.

I often told people around me, "Let me tell you the truth; I do not like how you did not do, say, or be." with an attitude full of expectation and blaming them for my unrest. I would put so much energy into pointing out others' flaws to show them they were wrong. It was like an entitlement to be their judge. How did I become this person? Should I have known better? Was I not a person of a pure heart? Did I mean well? What were my motives?

It all came down to my cultural conditioning; I was groomed for doom and imprisoned by believing the narrative passed down to me. I respect people who take the timeout and work on themselves because it is not easy to go against many of our ingrained beliefs and behaviors. It is, however, a necessary piece of the puzzle for finding peace.

This experience brought to life **Activating Inner Motivation (AIM)**, a concept I created to help us understand our struggles, manage our thoughts better, regulate our emotions, and challenge our beliefs. A chapter dedicated to this concept is further along in the book.

I thirst (GROW)

Not only was the situation suffocating and horrendous, but the thought of my husband not being by my side traumatized my codependent habit. Honestly, at that moment, I did not know what codependency was regarding the act itself. I just felt like my entire world came crashing down, and I could not do anything to change it. The best way to explain the feeling is like being dropped off in the ocean and not knowing how to swim: no lifeboat or rescue team--just tides, waves, and ripples. And you are told to learn to swim!

My emotional stability was unstable; I relied on my husband for emotional safety. Emotional codependency is an unhealthy relationship dynamic in which one person excessively relies on another for emotional support and a sense of identity. Codependent relationships can be emotionally and mentally draining, leading to resentment and anger. We have often heard the term, "She has a daddy issue." But what does this mean? Let's dive deep into my daddy issue.

Not getting attention from my dad at a young age led me to accept behaviors from others and myself that were not serving me, but instead, taking me on an emotional suffering path. This situation happens more often in a relationship or at home, where there is no awareness of emotional intelligence. Without any awareness, I was emotionally unstable. I carried the behavior over into my marriage, not just my marriage, but my job and external relationships.

It is important to point out that a healthy marriage or relationship is more stable when both individuals maintain their own healthy emotional identities and care for themselves first. If we are not careful, we focus on the other person's instability rather than demonstrating emotional *stability*. My husband and I had moments in our marriage where we demonstrated unhealthy behavior without the awareness of the consequences Our life experiences before we became a couple were different. We both had expectations of how our relationship should look and feel, which, for me, was influenced by TV sitcoms and my environment. I had so many cinematic expectations you would think we were *The Cosby Show*.

My environment was the building block of my belief system. I played the hero role, always trying to save the day with the best intentions. The hero always seemed to catch the villain and protect people from misfortune. I learned later that the underlying layer of being a hero is deactivating the other person's power, keeping them depending on you. A better approach would be modeling the way so that they can activate their willpower.

When a girl raises herself mentally, her way is the only way until something drastically crashes, or she opens her mind to something new. At the time of the bank robbery, even if someone on the outside looking in were to challenge my mindset, I could not receive it because I was closed-minded. Through my eyes, I wanted everything to go back to normal, whatever *normal* was for us.

When we married, my frame of mind was that I was giving my husband a gift—the gift of myself which he was supposed to accept just as I came. Broken, emotionally damaged, and social obscurity were just a few. My attitude was similar to the famous saying, "Love me for who I am"; however, I did not know who I was. So, basically, I wanted him to love and accept the idea of who I thought I was. Who I thought I was kept me stuck and paralyzed mentally.

My viewpoint was do not shake the gift box, do not dare try to open it--just leave it with the wrapping of all my past trauma and my distorted self-image. And please, be careful with me because you know I went through a rough time in my past, and I am not ready to leave there, but you can attend to my insecurities and rescue me from my fears by becoming my codependent partner in our unhealthy relationship. I am painting a picture of my mindset and how I viewed our agreement. The rule of the gift box was not only for my husband, but also for my work, friends, and family.

Being covered under a blanket of false identity created my fearful reality. Here, you had two people with two different perceptions of life. My perception was my reality; my reality was "my way was the right way, and his way was the wrong way." I am not referring to the bank robbery. My reality was a ten-year-old girl running from her past of sexual and emotional abuse. My molester had groomed me to believe his actions were normal; the worst part being the mental and emotional assault.

How does a ten-year-old person deal with pain, shame, and guilt? Well, let me tell you how I dealt with it. I became emotionally detached, stuck in my mind, and scared and afraid of living life. I was running from myself emotionally and even found myself running in my dreams at night. I wanted to escape from what I did not know how. I became a prisoner in my mind. I felt powerless with no protection. I wished my life were not mine. I hated myself for being me. My childhood died even with me still playing games with my friends and family. It felt like I was forced to carry the burden of my survival.

This ten-year-old girl got married inside a woman's body and looked at her marriage through the lens of familiar scenarios. Not knowing that deep beneath the beliefs of the victim's identity was pure love fighting for expression. Her battle between which identity got more attention became the dominant role in her marriage. Now, our marriage was at the mercy of what life brought next. Someone looking in would only see through what they had been exposed to regarding one's experience or perception.

The next day broke, and I finally got a call from my husband. I had no choice but to accept that I was a lone soldier.

Without actively trying to break my identity cycle, the unexpected drove a wedge in the middle, creating a breakout. I was left to ask myself questions I had never asked before and see possibilities I never thought to see before. *What's next? Would it be the grave, behind bars, or an unexpected miracle?* I hoped for an unexpected miracle, but the evidence was as objective as possible, proving it was time to go through the process.

Marriage is not a prison but a process. Knowing yourself is a process of having a relationship with God. Using the analogy of being processed when someone gets incarcerated, such as identifying who they are, taking fingerprints, pictures, etc., it is similar to entering a marriage, except they feel different, but both require a process. It is safe to say that marriage is a commitment to growth--where both individuals can shift and make changes. This can be problematic for some of us as it was for me for many years.

Marriage is ever-evolving because both individuals are growing, learning, and unlearning. Our marriage became the foundation that transformed my life. Only love is willing to create the space and time needed for our mental, emotional, and spiritual growth. Throughout the process, I followed my heart, even while ignoring my head, and it seemed like it was winning most of the time. The unquenched marriage thirst is a choice to let love lead the way. Love never fails.

CHAPTER TWELVE:
THE MIRROR OF SELF

How can you escape yourself when your world is in you?

We try to escape with whatever gives us some form of comfort. Comfort from outside yourselves will keep you looking outside of yourself extensively. Growing up, the church's fellowship was my happy place and comforted me. It gave me an outlet to shout out, cry, vent, hope, and wait for my rescuer. I created a belief that all my pain and suffering would be vindicated. I looked up at the sky and wondered when my time was coming. I waited for a long, long time until waiting became my norm. I was left to contend with my mind and memories, which I tried hard to block. I remember countless nights on the floor crying, screaming, begging. *Please, help me*, without saying it out loud for others to know. And then I turned around and comforted myself. *Do not worry; everything will be alright.*

My husband and I met while I was still in waiting mode. Our relationship was a sign my prayers were being answered. Life with us began with no guns and roses, just him giving me a reason to wake up my emotions. The little girl was still inside waiting, but I was ready to close that door and open another; well, that is what I thought. After the wedding, our baby arrived. I instinctively--by nature--began protecting her at all costs. The little girl inside me warned me daily to watch out for predators and wait to see if my newfound love would rescue her from her past.

Did God show up for me? Did my prayers get answered? Am I worth loving? Will he stay?

I reasoned that robbing a bank was not part of God's plan for our lives. *Could it have?* I thought! *How could I have gotten what I have been waiting so long to get snatched away without any explanation? Did I not cry hard enough? Did I not beg enough? Did I not follow the rituals? Did I not fast, pray, and serve enough?* The situation was taking me back to face the little girl inside me. She admitted that she had never stopped running, but I was willing to slow down, and was back on the track again.

Do you ever have dreams of yourself running? I used to dream of myself running for my life. No matter how the story goes in the dream, I am always running. Some people give meaning to their dreams, and some do not. At that time, I did not understand the dreams, but I hated the feeling I had while running for my life because it felt so real. Looking back now, I understand that it was the scared little girl inside me still running away from her life.

The things I consumed myself with over the years were not what I needed but what I wanted. I needed more. My shame was not enough for me; I needed more. My fears were not enough for me; I needed more. My distorted self-image was not enough for me; I needed more. My darkness was not enough for me; I needed more. My religion was not enough for me. The deeper I dug within myself, the more I understood I was not made for religion; religion was created for me. I was not made for this body; this body was created for me. I was not made for suffering; suffering was created as an experience.

Allow yourself to see and observe differently; being the observer generates new perspectives. -Stephanie Harrington

I did not understand how dopamine works in the human brain and how your environment can trigger the particular release of hormones associated with thoughts and beliefs. Beliefs shape thoughts, emotions, and actions. Actions then turn into habits and lifestyles. While going through the process of understanding myself, I realized that I created a belief that I was broken, lonely and a victim of shame and fear. My belief helped my thoughts and emotions, confirming that my screaming, crying, and begging for help and rescue is appropriate for emotional suffering.

We have often heard consistency is the key to success. Consistency is also the bed of despair. If every waking day you get up and reiterate the emotional suffering, you are being consistent. I used to believe I was not reiterating the emotional pain but overcoming the emotional suffering, and that is how I got stuck in the belief of overcoming. I stayed in that specific vibration and energy field. Accepting nothing more, nothing less. What is the difference between being on the bus and hoping to get off the bus? You are still on the bus.

My misconception of using my fellowship as a bandage to cover up a stabbed wound left me resentful. I also found comfort in things, hoping that I would find security. Such as a career that would give me financial freedom. Friends in high places, nice and fancy things. But what I needed was myself. It is like looking outside your window at everyone and everything passing by, hoping they would see you and rescue you from your home. You would think all you have to do is get up, open the door, and walk out.

Not when everyone outside is advertising all different types of narratives portraying fear and lack. They say that a life unobserved is not worth living. *Life is to be lived, not to be endured.* It is important to understand your mindset and learn what influences your decision-making. If something served you well or is still serving you, that's a keeper. If it did not serve you, that is something to be aware of and not let into your decision-making. We learn so much more about ourselves through reflection and self-evaluation.

When I started my business, networking and building relationships were the main components. I felt pumped and ready to connect whenever I got ready to attend a networking event. But fast-forward a couple of days in, and I was backing down by giving myself every reason why I shouldn't connect. This is not an issue to some who may not understand my reasoning. Using my new skill of asking myself questions and reflecting on past behavior, I understood that, unconsciously, I have a deeply-rooted belief that I might be a bother to people. I would talk myself out of connecting with others. I would justify the feeling with comments like, "I do not know what to say. What if I say the wrong thing?" I was afraid of sounding unprofessional and inexperienced, and I was scared of being humiliated or embarrassed. This was all because of my deep-rooted desire to be perfect. I constantly worried about being criticized for my performance. This feeling was a part of my everyday life.

I am a big believer in challenging your beliefs and changing your life. What if a belief could be the very thing standing in the way of you achieving a goal or a new lifestyle? Could challenging your beliefs give you a brand-new reality? Yes, it sure can. A belief is not permanent. It can be changed, but before we change them, we must first be aware of them. Self-reflection helps us observe our deep-rooted beliefs that are still the driving force behind many of our sufferings. Belief in expectations depletes your happiness, joy, and contentment. Belief in trying to control another person is a sure disappointment and can rob you of your time and attention.

I wished I could of just snapped my fingers and controlled my husband the day he got indicted for bank robbery. My controlling behavior was something I was practicing on him before the robbery without any awareness. A behavior I justified by my reasoning. It was like going to the ocean with a wicker basket and trying to fill the basket with water, hoping that every time I reached down to put more water inside the basket, the water would stay. All I wanted was for the water to stay in the wicker basket, just my little ounces of water, nothing more. All I wanted was my own family; that was my chase, and I was doing everything to hold it together and losing sight of the fact that I was trying to control the person by using guilt talk, manipulations, comparisons, and others' validations, trying to make a compelling case for my chase.

Think about a rat with cheese tied to a stick on its back and the cheese in front of it. All it sees is the cheese, not realizing the stick is connected to it and the distance between it and the cheese would always be the same. It does not know that it will never reach the cheese unless it stops and loses itself from the stick. My sticks were my expectations, fears, me running from my past pain, my what ifs, not trusting life, shame, worries, and so on.

What kind of sticks do you have tied on your back? The best way to find out is to look at your chase. What was your past like? What do you swear to yourself you will never do as they did? What makes you get angry quickly and strengthen your stick? Does it seem like you just have not quite gotten it as yet? Or perhaps it may be something you are still waiting to see happen in yourself or someone else. I see this behavior in parent-kid relationships, marriages, friendships, businesses, and families, addiction to drugs and food, and addiction to emotional suffering. The stick is always tied to your back, meaning that is the thing that is on your mind consistently. What do you think about the most? What do you give your attention and time to? What depletes you of your energy? What keeps you on a cycle?

The unrest mind is the string tied to the stick connected to the cheese. The string allows the cheese to go side to side, front to back, but can never be reached. So, what helps me break the stick of expectation, fear, what ifs, worries, and shame? What helped me was changing my mindset and challenging my beliefs about expectations, fears, what-ifs, and worries. I helped myself by changing my perception. With a changed mindset, there was no stick with cheese to chase. I ended the chase and started building my self-confidence, letting go of expectations, using fear as a tool, and allowing the what-ifs to be. I broke the stick by letting go of the deep-rooted belief I had buried. I broke the rules I had created and believed something different. Breaking the stick in your life may mean unlearning some things, stopping, and giving yourself attention rather than the cheese (chase).

The chase was created because I thought that was what I needed to fulfill my life. The chase comforted me with an expectation of a light at the end of the tunnel. My journey in life allowed me to experience a great career, own my own business, and achieve the American dream of a beautiful house. Despite these accomplishments, the stick was still tied to my back, and I created another chase, thinking it would be the next thing on the list. By breaking the stick of chase, I freed myself and invited presence, love, and appreciation of what was before me.

What is in front of me is the person looking back at me in the mirror. I love who I am—as-is--and recognize the beauty that lies within us, all the gifts of life, and the ability to channel creative energies in our experiences. The chase kept me trapped, tired, and unworthy. The mirror of self saved me from myself. I no longer criticize or judge myself. I am free from the chase to love who I am and build my life in love, not fear.

Faith is believing what you cannot see without having any evidence. You may not see or believe you are chasing something, but what is stealing your peace and joy? I, too, thought and believed my chase was the right thing until I became unrecognizable and confused. Self will never steer you in the wrong direction. I now know that our greatest destiny is self-discovery. Self-realization frees us from comparison, failure, and disappointment. All the expectations, fear, shame, and worries we put on ourselves deplete our energy and creativity.

You cannot escape yourself. You can, however, delay or deny yourself. But when you go to bed and wake up, the self is still waiting to be acknowledged and accepted. When we look somewhere else for what we need, we deny ourselves. There is nothing or no one better than you to live the life you were created to live. No fear, shame, expectation, or addiction can keep you from rising to the truth of who you are. What you see on the outside reflects what you are creating on the inside. Accepting self or not, you are who you are. You are a creator. Made from love and is love.

CHAPTER THIRTEEN:
EXTERNAL WEAPONS TO FIGHT INTERNAL WAR

Challenges Are Guides

Two days after the robbery, I stayed at my parent's house. And I was still in college with our 19-month-old baby. I did not have a plan. No job, no income. I had about four months left to finish my Bachelor's program, and I was determined to see it through. Those four months of school were the most challenging of the whole program. It was like life was saying, "Throw in the towel, let it be, and give up already!"

Do you find yourself using external weapons to fight an internal war? Well, you are not alone. Growth happens differently for many. In my early years, I focused more on physical development. I was more concerned with how I looked and felt based on what I saw. I struggled to lose weight as far back as I can remember. I would play the record each day whenever I had an encounter with food. My self-talk would remind me why I shouldn't be eating what I was eating but eating it anyway. I tried many diets and exercise plans but did not have any lasting change. It was not until I understood that my beliefs played a vital role in losing weight that I started seeing results.

Pain and struggle always ignite strength and courage in my mind. At the time, I considered myself spiritually mature. My energy stemmed from my faith and belief for the better, no matter what. The road was lonely and sad. Everyone seemed to be concerned, but not really. There was no genuine connection; it was more of *"Tell me your story,"* or *"Glad it's not me; sorry for you."* To be honest, it did not bother me then. I can admit now what I could not back then: I, too, like the attention. It is a hard truth to admit, but misery loves company. I played into toxic behaviors such as the "pity-party-save-me" syndrome. I did not know better. It seemed right at that time to identify with unhealthy behavior. I was modeling what was demonstrated to me without awareness or evaluation. It was not anyone's fault; everyone was doing the best they knew how to with what they were given or led to believe. That did not change the fact that I refused to accept any challenge. My daily aim was to find as much comfort as I could provide. Comfort in the way a narrative or a wish made me feel. My husband not being home made me feel abandoned, a feeling I did not know how to deal with. I bottled up all my anger and frustration and hid in shame, with only my body exposed to work and to provide for our child's needs.

I created opportunities by looking for what was better for us and going after it. It was terrifying, especially trying to figure things out alone without guidance; instead, I mainly had criticism. The pressure was real, and my mind was overloaded.

Overthinking became a regular pattern of mine. I spent most of my time in my head trying to figure things out, not letting go of anything. I would analyze every conversation and put meaning to each person's statement. This was not a good habit to develop, but I had been doing this for so long. It is just like any addiction; you want more and more and do not know how to stop. It is the same with overthinking. I would dig increasingly, contemplating a conversation and taking it way worse, like building a mountain out of a molehill. But I was trying to give myself meaning, something with which I could accept and live.

I vividly remember my mother's close friend who married a man from a different community. Being around them frequently as a child, I had the unique opportunity to overhear their conversations, even though they assumed I could not comprehend what they were discussing. Sadly, her husband consistently engaged in infidelity and compulsively denied wrongdoing. Whenever she approached my mother, seeking support in addressing his actions, my mother would agree to confront him. He stubbornly refuted the accusations, dismissing her as delusional and fabricating stories.

My mother's friend resorted to confiding in her husband's family, hoping they would intervene and convince him to change his ways. My mother's friend believed he might value their opinion and be more inclined to stop his behavior. Unfortunately, this approach proved futile, as the man remained undeterred. She felt utterly powerless, with her only defense being to seek solace in discussing the situation with his friends and relatives. Her mental well-being hinged on their responses. If they offered reassurances like, "Do not worry, all men cheat," she found temporary comfort in those words, allowing herself to find some semblance of peace within that confined space. Alternatively, they might have said things like, "He loves you." "He constantly talks about you," or "You are the only one for him." Witnessing this pattern throughout my upbringing seemed like a way to pacify someone trapped in an invisible prison serving a mental sentence. The more she dwelled on the issue, the larger it loomed in her mind. It reached a point where every interaction with my mother's friend revolved solely around her and her husband's dysfunctional relationship; it consumed her thoughts akin to an addiction.

I became consumed by relentless overthinking, constantly trying to decipher the intentions of those around me. This tendency stemmed primarily from deep-rooted trust issues, making it incredibly challenging to open up to others. I would meticulously analyze and assign meaning to the things I did not fully comprehend, perpetually seeking to unravel the motives behind people's actions.

I had yearned for a life of smooth sailing, but circumstances took an unexpected turn. My husband found himself incarcerated, and as a result, I found myself submerged in a sea of financial debt and emotional sorrow. I had no choice but to make ends meet, so I pushed myself to the limit, juggling multiple jobs just to cover the necessary expenses for my daughter. My days became a routine around work, church, and the endless cycle of my repeated actions.

My social life became non-existent as I had no time or energy to spare. Instead, I would spend most of my days lost in my thoughts, desperately trying to navigate the aftermath of my tragedy and devise a survival plan.

Living paycheck to paycheck feels like tying a fragile limb of a tree to a goat, unsure when it would give way and desperately hoping it would not. This struggle becomes even more daunting when a family depends on you. During this period, I worked as a school nurse in the morning and attended to extended care duties in the evening. This meant my baby was dropped off at daycare early in the morning and picked up as the last child at night. By the time we arrived home, darkness had enveloped the outside world, signaling bedtime. This cycle repeated itself daily, leaving little space for deep emotional connection. Our focus was primarily on meeting basic needs and providing for survival. It often felt like I was raising a resilient little soldier as my daughter stood alongside me in the battle against adversity.

At every step of the way, she was my constant companion. Our mother-daughter bond grew stronger with each passing day. As a young child, I witnessed my mother's unwavering efforts to provide for our family. Though my understanding of life was limited at that tender age, I felt a compelling urge to rescue my mom. I wanted to be her savior, granting her the freedom to soar above the burdens she carried. Seeing her shed tears as helplessness stripped away her power pained me. I carried a heavy load, grappling with the weight of molestation, the profound abandonment that comes from growing up without a father, and the perpetual feeling of being an outsider within our large family.

I embarked on a quest to build my own family, convinced I deserved happiness and fulfillment. Life, however, seemed to have plans, serenading me with a different melody from the one I had envisioned. I saw a reflection of my mother in my eyes, seeing my daughter witnessing her mother's tears as she fought to survive. Though I found myself in a different country, at a different time, and facing different circumstances, I could not help but notice the echoes of my mother's struggles resurfacing in my life. My only advantage was that my daughter was younger than I was when I first formed my perceptions. This allowed me the precious window of time to break the cycle and create something entirely different.

I faced numerous challenges in my life, including living conditions, finances, and overall peace of mind. I yearned for change, a fresh start that would allow me to escape from my past and venture into the unknown, where no one knew my story. Embracing this change meant embarking on the journey alone, stepping into unfamiliar territory again. But the desire for transformation outweighed any lingering shame, propelling me forward.

With my daughter by my side, I relocated to a new area up North, armed with one friend on whom I could rely. Temporarily, we stayed with her and her family until I could secure our place. It took approximately two months for me to adjust to this unfamiliar town. Despite being a married woman navigating the challenges of single parenthood, I managed to secure a job as a certified nursing assistant at a local hospital, despite holding a bachelor's degree in Nuclear Medicine with no experience in the field. While it may not have been my ideal job, it provided the means to sustain ourselves until I could establish a more stable foundation.

On my first day of orientation at the hospital, misfortune struck me as my car broke down on the side of the road. Thankfully, it happened near the hospital, allowing me to walk there. I contacted a tow truck company to retrieve the car and transport it to a mechanic for repairs. As I walked to the hospital, a wave of overwhelming emotions washed over me, and tears streamed down my face. Life felt unbearably tricky then, and I longed to escape it all.

As I sat in the orientation meeting, I was drawn to the scene unfolding outside the window, the sight of my car being loaded onto the tow truck. Panic surged as I realized the tow truck driver required the key to proceed. Feeling urgent, I hastily excused myself from the meeting and rushed to the nearest elevator. With a hint of desperation, I went down to street level and handed over the car key to the tow truck driver, as my anxiety was palpable in the air.

Uncertainty loomed over me as I pondered how to get home or even make it to my second day of work without a functional car. Once the orientation concluded, I stepped outside and immediately contacted my friend for assistance; however, she was still at her workplace, leaving me with no immediate means of transportation. I found solace under the shade of a nearby tree, patiently waiting for hours until she finished her shift and could come to pick me up.

Eventually, my friend arrived, and we stopped at the mechanic's shop to assess the car's condition. To my dismay, I received the disheartening news that the car was plagued with electrical problems, requiring an expensive repair costing $850. At that moment, I only possessed $700, which was meant to sustain us until I received my first paycheck. The financial gap left me feeling overwhelmed, uncertain how to bridge it while meeting our immediate needs.

I mustered up the courage and approached the mechanic shop owner, explaining my financial constraints and proposing dividing the payment into three manageable installments. To my surprise and relief, the owner agreed to accommodate my request. Despite my challenges, I smiled and focused on my new job, determined to make the most of the opportunity.

My next hurdle was enrolling my daughter in VPK (Voluntary Pre-Kindergarten), but unfortunately, her birth date fell after the September cut-off, making her ineligible. It felt as if all my carefully laid plans were crumbling before my eyes, and a sense of being cursed started to creep into my thoughts. With the added expense of childcare, concerns about affording our apartment and putting food on the table weighed heavily on my mind. The prospect of returning home and confronting my perceived failures became an agonizing decision to contemplate. I could not help but feel like I had let my daughter down.

In search of a solution, I made the tough choice to send my daughter to stay with my mother-in-law for a month or two until my mother could join me from Jamaica to lend a helping hand. This decision weighed heavily on my heart. With my husband imprisoned, and my daughter sent away, no vibrant rainbow in the sky granted me a favor. Instead, dark clouds of regret and shame overshadowed my thoughts.

Letting go of my child was an indescribable pain for a mother. She was just a little girl, innocent and vulnerable. I felt a surge of anger, overwhelmed by my lack of control over the situation. Nevertheless, I would try to convince myself that it would be temporary and that I needed to stay focused on the mission ahead.

I toiled tirelessly, accepting any job opportunity that came my way, regardless of the time or nature of the work. Each day, I made it a point to call and speak with my daughter, seeking solace in our conversations. The weight of frustration and anguish was overwhelming, surpassing the mere act of crying. I felt like a ticking time bomb, almost exploding with pent-up emotions. I despised every aspect of my life while simultaneously seeking solace in my faith, hoping that God would intercede on my behalf, perhaps sending some heavenly blessing of financial relief.

Under the relentless grip of change, my temperament turned bitter, devoid of taste or appeal. It seemed as though everything I held dear had been torn away from me, leaving me stripped of dignity, self-esteem, and any remnants of honor. My deepest longing was for my family, who had become my idol, only to be cruelly snatched away. Helplessness consumed me, and I found myself grasping for reasons to justify why I deserved their presence. Born from pain, my upbringing was steeped in suffering, and now I had inadvertently constructed a family forged in the crucible of pain. Yet, amidst it all, I could not shake the persistent feeling that I did not deserve the hardships unfolding in my life.

I have since realized that placing something or someone above yourself can be addictive, like a drug that consumes you entirely. My family became that potent drug, and I was willing to sacrifice everything for its sake. I failed, however, to recognize that this intense focus on my family came at a cost, the cost of passing down unhealthy behavior patterns to my daughter.

If I did not clean up my act, I would burden her with my emotional baggage instead of providing her with the valuable lessons that would nurture her growth and resilience. I needed to shift from a victim mentality to one of character-building and inner strength, ensuring that she could absorb the valuable nutrients of wisdom and experience.

It was my responsibility to go through and grow through the patterns passed down through generations. We do not just escape or run from family traits; we deal with them by uncovering the truth that lies beneath our pain. Breaking the suffering victim mindset of what I was running from not only saved me but also set up the next generation of women in my family to believe in themselves and see life obstacles as challenges to build, grow, and shine.

We all possess a vital tool: our mind. Utilizing the power of our mind helps us harness its potential for positive growth. My daughter does not see me struggling; she sees me facing challenges and becoming a better person and a woman she can be proud of. The external weapon of covering up and trying to get through life differs from the proper mindset to fight the internal battle of self-control and discipline.

Discipline is not a consequence of what happens to us but a choice to do better and become better. I can write it out or shout it out that my life circumstances were someone else's fault, but all I would be doing is setting up my daughter to fail. Children do not do what you tell them to do they do what they see you do. We cannot continue to fight our internal battle with external weapons such as looking strong and pretending to be confident under our makeup and apparel. It must be authentic from within.

The battle daily is for our mind, our attention, and time. What we give attention to grows bigger and louder in our minds, family, and community. I used what I saw my mother used to fight her battle--I complained, I cried, and sought pity. But only to end up with the same result as my mother, who was just getting by. I had to accept myself as who God intended for me to be when He thought of me. And I had to be the one who defeated the generation's blindness to self.

Your freedom frees you, your family, and the generations to come. You are the one chosen to break generational blindness. We are in the age of information, so we have the tools to do the work within. Pointing fingers and blaming a system, a person, or a thing is still a coverup for fear and unacceptance. I shared my many misfortunes and the mindset I accepted, which I believed created more of what I did not want.

Accepting myself, my calling, and my purpose helps me and my family profit abundantly. I encourage you to look within and face yourself while winning your internal fight. In the end, you will discover you are the key component in the fight. Your past generation does not define you; it is you who defined yourself. Your challenges are your guide to go deeper.

CHAPTER FOURTEEN:
WHICH NARRATIVE ARE YOU AFFIRMING?

Each day, I fixated on my problems, giving them unwavering attention. I would engage in endless conversations with others, rehashing the woes of my life as if I were on a constant loop. Even in prayer, whether alone or with spiritual leaders, I would pour out my grievances, recounting the hardships that plagued my family and me. Every sad event and every setback were meticulously documented in my journal as if to solidify the narrative of my suffering.

My heart grew heavier daily with a cocktail of emotions: shame, fear, worry, and an overwhelming sense of powerlessness. These emotions fed into my belief that I was merely a victim, reinforcing that perspective daily.

My mind meticulously documented every detail as if I were the self-appointed observer of my oppression. I had internal cloud storage where I uploaded every hardship and every struggle. Doubt and insecurities consumed me, and they found their way into the emails I sent, filled with my innermost vulnerabilities, expressing my uncertainties. The subject line of these messages could read:

I am the victim.

Help me,

I am poor; I barely have enough.

I have a degree, but no one will hire me because I have no experience.

I have to take what I get.

I have to do what I have to do.

That's not for me; that's for them.

I wish I had.

I wish I could.

I have no money. I am broke.

They will never pick me.

It's because I am black.

I am oppressed.

I am broken.

I am lost.

I cannot survive this one.

Life is too hard.

I do not have the time to do that.

I cannot afford that.

That is too much money for me.

I need a word.

I do not have the brains for that.

I cannot lose weight.

I tried everything, but nothing works.

I worry too much.

I have no patience for that.

Satan is strong.

The devil is trying his hardest to destroy me.

I have no peace in this house.

My whole life is a mess.

I trust no one.

No one has my best interest at heart.
Nobody loves me.
Nobody cares for me.
Everyone just stresses me out.
The struggle is real.

I created my dark cloud. Using my most valuable possession and planting new seeds each time, I affirmed what I did not want. I was the builder and upholder of the life I was running from. The subconscious mind does not know the difference between right and wrong; it just manifests what is planted as fruits. In the dark cloud of my mind, I had acres of the damaging crops ready for harvest. My circumstance or current situation was the fruit of the tree of darkness, even though I would like to think that was not my intention because my motives were pure, and all I wanted was freedom from suffering. Like attracts like. Suffering attracts suffering. Emotional pain attracts more emotional pain. Ignorance attracts more ignorance. Fear attracts fear. Abundance attracts abundance, which explains why the rich are more prosperous and the poor poorer.

The subconscious does not respect a person's things or what is asked. Ask, and it gives. Seek, and you find. Knock, and it opens. I asked for what I did not want by affirming what I did not want and finding what I did not want. I sought for more reasons to prove I was a victim, and I found more reasons to prove I was a victim. I knocked on the door to understand why my life was how it was, opening up more understanding of why it was the way it was.

It is easier to put a puzzle together when you have an image of the bigger picture in your mind. If the image in your mind is broken, oppressed, or victimized, the puzzle pieces will be assembled to fit the image. If the image in your mind is happy, healthy, and wealthy, then it is easier to put those pieces of the puzzle to fit the image. If you have no image, you have a clean slate to create whatever you wish to create freely.

I was told many times I was too gullible. I took what I saw around me at face value and ran with it. When I allowed myself to take on a victim's role or the sufferer, I always looked for an attacker, someone, or something to blame. That took all my attention away from looking at myself; instead, I looked at others. I blamed all the people that hurt me. I blamed my challenges. I blamed organizations that promote mass media marketing. I blamed different persuasive storytellers. I blamed my husband for why my dream died. I blamed fear and shame for holding me back. I blamed molestation. I blame cultural differences. I blamed societal expectations. And the list went on.

When I had nothing left to blame, I was left with MYSELF! I had no choice but to face the woman in the mirror. Taking responsibility for accepting my life as my doing is not what I wanted to believe. What was looking back at me in the mirror was my choice. Yes, the choices I made were influenced by others. But the understanding that I am the author and creator, good or bad, deactivated my suffering. I realized that my entire life was accepting a belief about myself and then trying to prove to the world that the belief I wore was not my identity.

In my quest to assign blame to the outside world, I found myself trapped in a cycle of proving my worth to others. There was a deep longing to showcase my strength as if to say, "Look, I have overcome! Look at what you did to me." This need for external validation became a desperate plea for attention.

I eventually came to a profound realization; I needed to be honest with myself and develop deeper within, seeking validation from within rather than from external sources. It was time to dispel the illusions I had created and confront the truth. I was never truly broken, oppressed, or a victim, but my belief in these falsehoods made them a reality.

In this process of self-discovery, I uncovered the strength and resilience that had continuously resided within me. I no longer needed to deceive myself or seek validation from others. The only person I needed to prove myself to was myself, reaffirming my true essence and recognizing that I was never defined by the illusions I had once believed.

Every challenge in life is a matter of perspective, and I used to perceive every challenge as the work of the devil. I would sing along to the famous song "The Devil Is a Liar" to cope with and dismiss my difficulties. It was enough to get through the day. I constantly analyzed and reflected on my actions, continually seeking improvement; however, deep down, I believed I was always right. This mindset, though implied, shaped my perspective during that phase of my life.

In my journey, I fell into the same trap as Eve, being deceived by what caught my eye. I focused on the external world, relying on what was presented rather than looking within the depths of my being. I allowed the opinions and teachings of others to infiltrate my mind, embracing various doctrines that attempted to define who I truly am. But the truth is, no one, not even myself, can fully define my essence. I am infinite, beyond definition and limitation.

Every day presents an opportunity to shape my narrative and rewrite my story. By changing the words I speak and believe, I can transform my reality. I am the author of my existence, constantly evolving and growing. Embracing this truth empowers me to break free from the constraints of external influences and discover the boundless potential within me.

Regardless of what I say to you, the reader, about your infinite nature, your response and acceptance of it depend on the narratives you have heard and internalized throughout your life. I could attempt to define you, and you could try to define yourself, but ultimately, you are beyond definition. Embracing this truth can be challenging because we often seek a sense of belonging. We accept the narrative that we should fit in somewhere. Consider this: if we did not belong, why are we here?

Just as your fingers are connected to your arm because that is where they belong, and your neck is connected to your head because that is where it belongs, you are here because this is where you belong. It is the natural order of things. We do not see teeth on fingers or necks on feet because they do not belong there. The same principle applies to your existence. Your uniqueness and purpose are intertwined with the place and space you inhabit. Any specific mold or category does not define you; you are here uniquely.

Our minds are exposed to different ideologies. To relate to the question asked in the ancient text, *"Who told you that you were naked?"* is for us to THINK. Who told you that you were a victim, who told you were oppressed, who told you those toxic deep-rooted beliefs? Who told you your social status? Who told you what is wrong and what right is? Who told you who you are? No one can define you. You are undefinable.

You do not have to wear anyone's labels. Getting rid of the fig leaves syndrome can be challenging if you do not know you are covered under one. I did not realize that what kept fear alive in my life was that I believed in fear. I served fear by affirming daily all the things that could go wrong in my life. To be honest, this is not a truth I wanted to believe. But accepting is believing, and believing is creating.

I used to believe in feeling fear. I used to believe in feeling suffering. I made it real by "feeling it." I kept it alive. The feeling is believing. The more I give that thought attention, the more it replicates itself in a

The more I give that thought attention, the more it replicates itself in a different form.

different form. It may manifest as a car accident. Or lost a job, creating more fear about bills. Behind the physical is energy, and energy attracts like energy. The energies that served me then did not serve me well.

Because my focus was external, my choices also were exterior. I was looking at what was already the result of a manifestation. It is like looking at the stock market charts. The candle sticks on the left show you what has already taken place over the different periods, which gives you analytical and statistical data to back-test and create a new strategy to execute good trades based on patterns and behavior of the market. If you do not know why your choices affect you, you will likely do the same thing repeatedly. The energy behind the physical is attracting the same energy, replicating itself.

It is essential to understand that our desire is always leading the way. Desires that serve us well and desires that do not serve us are fueled by attention. It took years for me to realize the hard way of life without knowledge or experience. I gave the attention I did not want. Did you notice I said, "I *gave*"? That means I was *giving*. Give, and it will come back to you. Not only good intentions but hostile intentions will come back to you. It is like saying we get what we deserve because we first send out that intention.

Every day is the first day.

The beauty of nature is that no one controls the narrative. Look at the sun, moon, trees, ocean, and mountains. You can tell what is real and what is an illusion.

Nature has no hidden agenda and no need to convince anyone to believe the sun is the sun or the moon is the moon. It is what it is.

I knew I could not do anything to change the outcome of my husband's arrest, but I sure wished I could. Our lives were at the mercy of the law, and he had to serve his time based on his crime. It is the same when breaking free from your old self, emotional patterns and behaviors, thought processes, and actions. You will go through a season of experiencing what you have already created; you have to serve the time according to the universal law, but it is important not to give up on yourself because your new day is coming. All you need is time. Time helps us prove our worth, values, and commitment to personal growth. In the ancient text, there is a verse that states, "Prove me, O Lord, and try me: test my heart and mind" (Proverbs 26:2).

My self-discovery journey led me to fully understand what waiting is and who I was waiting on in terms of creating from within. It is the time to prove to ourselves that we can do exceedingly abundantly above all we can ever ask or imagine. We can create happy emotions, feelings of ease, and true acceptance because we are conscious creators living our best lives as promised. Let today be your first day. Do not worry if you mess up every day. It can be your first day, as it was for me until I started to see the fruit of my tree. The crime I committed was the negative self-talk, the distorted self-image, and the emotional and mental trauma. I sure did serve my time in my mental prison, as did my husband in the physical prison.

Time helps us prove that we deserve God's goodness. But it is up to us to go deeper and open the vault inside us all. Whether your crime is against yourself or others, time will give you every waking morning to prove the cause to yourself or them. My husband robbing a bank was a federal crime against the laws of our nation, but the man who committed the crime had and has something to prove.

What was there to prove? The crime committed? The man behind the wall? The intentions? The character? The perception? The beliefs? Or the conditioned mindset?

I will let him share that with you in a later chapter.

I knew I had a choice to make. Every day was the first day that allowed me to unlearn and rewrite a new script for my life. I practice mirroring the walls in my life. Looking closely, I ask:

- *What are my struggles?*
- *What wall do I keep hitting against?*
- *Why did I build those walls?*
- *Was the wall protecting me by keeping others out or keeping me in?*
- *What conversation or topic seems complicated to address?*
- *What difficulties am I facing when I enter a room?*
- *Why am I afraid to speak my mind?*
- *What invisible wall is preventing me from expressing my true nature?*

I built an invisible wall only I could feel. These walls were not seen; they were felt. And sometimes, when they spoke, they may have said, "I do not feel like I can do that." It was never if it *were* a possibility, it was more of my invisible not feeling the possibility.

What invisible wall do you have right now that is blocking your view? How do you see yourself? How do you feel about yourself? How do you face that wall? My invisible walls never constantly exposed their length or the width of their dimensions, but what I always felt caused my reaction.

You probably never stop to think about whether you have any invisible walls, but the purpose of walls is to shut things out and protect you from getting hurt. The brain does a great job protecting you, but protection sometimes comes at a cost. Like the concept seen in some Mafia movies: they break your window then tell you to pay them to protect you. I build my invisible walls, then I turn around and hide inside and blame others to pay the price of me not being myself when all I had to do was break the walls down.

How do I break down the invisible walls?

First, I began to turn my attention inward, focusing on my mind, the builder, my most prized possession. I call the mind the lighthouse, the sweet spot of transformation where shifts happen. It is my birthright to use my mind to serve me. But it was an undisclosed choice of which I was not aware. Consciously choosing and not consciously choosing is still choosing. I had to choose between remaining bandaged up or freeing myself from what I did not want for myself.

Freedom comes at the price of losing everything: all the expectations, ideas, perceptions, attachments, and the music in the background. Freedom asks me the question: *Is there not a cause?* Yes, there is. Me. You. I am worth freely creating with the understanding of what I am creating. You are worth it. They are worth it. We are worth it. Humanity is helping humanity by bringing more self-awareness and understanding of oneself.

A new day is a clean slate, allowing the artist to be creative and take inspired action daily. A new day might be a new season, chapter, or beginning. My experience taught me I was always creating. Someone's trash is someone else's treasure. What I created before with my life is now being used to build the minds of others.

I need to be mindful of my actions and energy. Everything we do and say can impact those around us, both physically and energetically. The concept of "no one left behind" emphasizes that we should strive to be inclusive and considerate of others. It encourages us to be intentional with our thoughts, emotions, and beliefs.

By being mindful of our energy and its impact on others, we can cultivate more positive and compassionate relationships and create a more harmonious world. In a rapidly changing world, adaptability and openness to new ideas and ways of thinking are essential. By embracing change and being willing to learn and grow, we can create a better future for ourselves and future generations.

I have primarily worked as a Nuclear Medicine Technologist throughout my medical career. My work has involved using radiopharmaceuticals and radioisotopes to illuminate the physiology of various organs during diagnostic procedures. This aspect of my work has always fascinated me, as it provides a window into the unseen workings of the body.

Interestingly, life has a way of connecting what is seen with what is unseen. During specific diagnostic procedures, we inject the radioisotope into the patient being imaged under a gamma camera, allowing us to observe the flow of radioisotopes in the bloodstream and illuminate the function of specific organs.

Similarly, our intentions can create a flow of energy that illuminates different parts of our minds, allowing us to manifest the things we truly desire for ourselves. I like going behind the scenes and writing the script before it is played out in our lives. We can create a more fulfilling and purposeful life by being intentional with our thoughts and actions.

CHAPTER FIFTEEN:
FACING YOUR FEELINGS FROM WITHIN

"Gettin' real with it."

You cannot fix what is not broken.

Every day, I used to use my mind to deep dive into different worst-case scenarios that could happen. I did not know I was building a prison in my mind. I did not know we become what we believe. I did not know I was doing more harm than good to myself and my family. I did not know I would create what I did not want due to my thoughts. I would not want anyone to see some of the thoughts I had if they were to be played on screen.

I was utterly reckless in my thinking. It had been like that as far as I can remember. I chose to think those unwanted thoughts--a hard truth to accept. I taught myself to think I was a bother to people and that no one cared about me. I told myself people only wanted me around to use me. I told myself I should feel sorry for myself and other people should pity me. I told myself I would be vindicated based on my perception of the narrative to wait on God. I told myself I needed a pastor or a spiritual leader to give me a word or pray for me to feel good about my life. I told myself that was what God wanted for me. I told myself to give others more of my time and attention because it sounded good and looked good, not understanding that I needed to give to myself first before I could genuinely give to others.

I was the liar, the thief, and the destroyer in my life. In the Bible John 10:10 says, "The thief comes only to kill, steal, and destroy." I was the very thing hurting myself with no awareness. I played defense against myself, thinking I was living a righteous life, not realizing I was like a cancer cell eating away at itself. I did not know I was living a mediocre lifestyle. I honestly believed my lies. My motive, however, was to be a good person, and I wanted to make my family, friends, myself, and God happy by doing the right thing. And by the right thing, I mean the righteous follower of Christ. Keep His commandment, live peacefully, and witness to others about love and heaven. I devoted my entire life to this way of living without understanding what Christ meant, where heaven and hell were, and who God is.

To have faith was to accept a narrative and just believe it—this is what my perception was. I truly believed from the depths of my soul that is what the God of the universe wanted for me. Based on this foundation, I made all my decisions, reasoning, and lifestyle. Religion was taught to me, and I followed the rituals and participated fully in the operations. At fifteen years old, my grandmother and some church members took us to a river to be baptized. That day was so tranquil and refreshing. It felt like I was committing to something big, and everyone was very proud of me. Especially God, I thought; I was showing Him that I wanted to be his servant and be obedient to His will. My grandmother was a local preacher, and our lives were built around religion and service to the church and community. I remember thinking this was the best decision I had ever made, and I would prove to God how much I love Him. It felt good, like a release from stress and much of a burden. *Now, I have someone in my corner.*

After being baptized, I was told I needed to be more serious about my new life, which entails reading the bible, attending services, and participating in the workings of the church. This was easy for me. I love serving people; I love to see people's lives get better. With little understanding of setting boundaries and the need for acceptance, I became a people pleaser, which did more harm than good in my personal life. I was told to be different from the people in the world by looking different, dressing differently, and not participating in anything outside of the Christian cultural expectations. From my understanding, we must show others how God's people look and act.

Now, at this time in my life, I lived in a small country town and was not exposed to the world around me. As I got older and became more involved in my spiritual growth, I became more active in church as a singer on the praise team, a Sunday school teacher, and sometimes an usher. I was always fascinated by the stories and the characters, especially the ones that pointed out God's chosen people. This attitude spiked my ego because I believed I was doing what God wanted. I felt like I was special and might be rewarded for being obedient. I dedicated my entire life to the service of God and the Christian Religion. I would only miss a service or a function if it were out of my control. I prided myself on being a good servant leader and believed my place in heaven was secure.

By the time I was nineteen years old, I had migrated to the United States. After leaving my hometown congregation and living across the ocean, I needed to plug into another church. There was no escaping it, especially from my grandmother; I was asked in every phone conversation we had, *"Did you find a church yet?"*

One of my family members here in the States invited me to a Jamaican church she and her family attend. They were called the Church of God, which meant to me at that time that they believed in the Holy Spirit and spoke in tongues and holier. This way of worship differed from what I was used to in Jamaica. I grew up in a quieter and more reserved Methodist church, with no dancing, jumping, shaking, twirling, or spinning. Service always ends on time; they go through a schedule that is replicated weekly. I have heard people call my church the dead church with no life. But that was all I knew growing up,

I was in a new environment and needed to learn their ritual and ways of worship. They had no sense of time; the church could run from three to five hours. I was told it depended on "how the Spirit leads." I knew nothing about the Holy Spirit because I had never encountered the Spirit. I was told I needed to be baptized again and filled with the Holy Spirit. I ran with that narrative and submitted myself to the teaching because I did not want to miss out on being an honest Christian on fire for God. I would sing, dance, and worship God; by the end of the service, I was tired and drained of energy.

My life entirely revolved around my church; nothing outside could penetrate my mindset and belief system, and once I learned to use the name of Jesus at the end of anything, that set the stage to make things work in my favor. I did not question the meaning or the logic behind most of the things I learned because that would mean I was going against God. Months after months, I kept attending church and getting more involved. I am in another country around other people in the world. One of our teachings is to be different from the people in the world. We must be different, act different, and look different. I did not specifically know who the people were or what they looked like to fit the description, which implied evil, wickedness, and not sons of God because people were everywhere in the grocery store, school, and work environment. How can you tell if they are of the world or not? My ignorance, caused by my lack of knowledge, made me judge and criticize others based on how they look, act, or carry themselves. I would judge people through my eyes based on what I believed was right or wrong. If it was someone I witnessed, and they seemed to be in distress, I would encourage them that they needed Jesus and should come as they are because Jesus would not refuse them. I would be persistent and tell them what they needed and how to get it. My method of helping was beating people up with scripture and reassuring them how hot hell is.

Some people listen and go to church; some do not. I felt good believing I did the right thing and was building God's kingdom. I believed this was my purpose and ran with all my heart and will. I never missed out on a conference or any power hours created to usher in the presence of God. By now, you can tell I was devoted.

Living with my dad sometimes meant peaches and cream or bitter water. My family had different commitments to different places of worship. My dad is a Jehovah's Witness; my stepmother is a Seventh-day Adventist; and I was in the Church of God. We all believe the church we attend is the real one, and that is where God's spirit dwells. I remember my little sister being torn between who she should go to church with and not making anyone feel bad. Can you imagine our conversation at the dinner table? There was always a seat for God and the Devil; they never missed a meal. Most of the time, they eat most of the food, leaving us empty and divided. Food was on the table, but we were still hungry and thirsty. That was all we knew: how to curse ourselves with our words and try to prove the unprovable. We used our beliefs to beat down and build each other up. The two-course meal involved "God's always teaching a lesson" and "The devil is always on the side that does not go in that person's favor." I battled religion at home and outside of the house, in the church, and the people in the world.

There is a language that we sometimes reiterated daily in our home:

- "The devil is a liar."
- "I rebuke you."
- "Get behind me, Satan."
- "God is turning things around."
- "God is watching us."
- "Look what God is going to do."
- "God is waiting on the right time."
- "You need to listen."
- "It may be too late."

There was never a day that passed that someone did not utter one of these phrases. When the conversation did not go in our favor, we assured ourselves God's timing is right timing or comfort ourselves with anything that sounds like what we think God wants us to hear.

I became an expert in using my religion as a weapon to block myself from feeling or dealing with an emotion or situation I did not want. I would remind myself that the devil is at work and trying to take me out, but God will not allow it. Here I was, a young lady in a new city, battling the fear of not making it to heaven, fighting the devil, trying to be strong for God, pushing myself to get an education, and running from the emotional pain of the distorted self-image. My self-image was not what I looked like outside because I did everything to look good, but rather how I felt inside. Hair was always done, clothes on fleek, nails and accessories were never an issue; modesty was my dress code. I never felt I was not good enough; no, I felt like I was not *seen*; no one saw me or acknowledged me. I felt insignificant and unappreciated, and I longed for attention and the warmth of love inside.

When my husband and I got married, we were both young and still learning about the world around us. You may ask, *What would you have done differently?* If this question were asked to me while going through the process at that particular time, I would have said, "I wouldn't want to feel those feelings again. Especially the feeling of exiting my skin."

Let me explain: not only was I battling emotional pain, the color of my skin was also under attack. I am a black woman, and my skin color was perceived as a threat in the world in which I had been born. Looking back, I sometimes missed out on many opportunities or experiences due to my preoccupation with waiting for something to change or someone to rescue me from myself.

Today, I say the emotional trauma I experienced robbed me of some of life's experiences. Still, it has also given me valuable lessons and data on how to make better choices in my life and, in the same vein, share my experience with millions of people around the globe.

Our experiences serve as a valuable currency that we can use to build our future selves. But it took self-reflection to see what worked for me and what did not. I paid the price for the knowledge I now have of my life. It cost me something. I endured life's colorful wheel blindly following and scared of making my own decisions. I looked at others instead of the role I played in my life. But honestly, even if I were told to switch roles, I still would not believe or accept it because, deep down--where the first seed was planted--had to be acknowledged and replaced. I first believed in a savior and being a humble servant and a follower, so waiting superseded any other reasoning.

I used my mind to deceive myself, becoming my own worst enemy. I fell into the trap of embracing delusions and convincing myself of their truth. I adopted the role of a victim, allowing life to play the role of the villain. By shutting off my emotions, I inadvertently drained my emotional reserves. In my pursuit of becoming a strong and resilient woman capable of handling anything, I unintentionally suppressed my genuine emotions, hindering my ability to connect with others and express my creativity from within. While

I may be inclined to blame teachers or my environment, it is ultimately through my mind that everything passes. I am the gateway through which all experiences flow.

Even though I am proud of myself for pushing through and overcoming myself, I now realize that it came at a high cost, a price I paid, a price many others have paid and are still paying. To reap the benefits, I must die to my old thinking and arise with a new mindset.

God is love. Love is God. I am the church. My new mindset is founded upon this belief, tested and tried. I am evolving to love, growing, and expanding my awareness. There is no life without death, and vice versa, and there is no death without life. The law of polarity states that everything happens in duality. It is like meeting a newer version of myself and trusting, rebuilding, and acknowledging my essence. Feel the feeling and deal with it because I can.

My recovery phase was just as challenging as blocking my unwanted feelings in the first place. Our feelings are crucial in connecting with others and remembering our past experiences. Despite being told not to trust our feelings, I believe in listening to my feelings because they often communicate something important. My feelings were telling me that I was in a dark place, a dark place, meaning a lack of knowledge and understanding and creating a low-energy field. Instead, I ignored my feelings by blaming an external entity or a person, not knowing I created my feelings. I did not know this truth at that time of my journey. I have suppressed my feelings with hope without taking action and spending time listening to myself. I avoided experiencing the uncomfortable emotions I did not want to feel and did not examine them on a deeper level.

Where I stand today, I understand that acknowledging and examining those unwanted feelings is crucial for transforming them into higher-energy feelings. To create this requires me to spend time with myself and embrace all my emotions, even the difficult ones. Everyone's response to life experiences is unique. Our fears and worries differ from person to person. Still, they all stem from memory, maybe from a traumatic experience or through building our perception. All at the same time, creating an emotion that associates the feeling with the situation. It does not matter, the catalyst.

For example, during challenging times, I often turn to a specific song as a coping mechanism, while someone else may listen to the same song for an entirely different purpose. Although the song remains unchanged, our emotions and energy levels differ due to our unique thoughts and feelings. Occasionally, certain songs evoke specific emotions, but only if we grant them our attention. I select particular songs to boost my energy or to induce a state of relaxation and tranquility. It revolves around the song's lyrics, which resonate with our thoughts and align with the musical frequency. Ultimately, we must attribute meaning and significance to the song or music we encounter.

Therefore, it is not healthy to compare ourselves to others. I used to judge others based on my experience of emotional suffering, assuming that what I felt was the same as what others were feeling. This perspective made me criticize and misinterpret others' actions as if looking through my brokenness or limited beliefs. When I shifted my perspective and viewed things differently, I began to see the world differently.

This transformative shift occurred solely because I decided to question my beliefs. I challenged my notions about myself, my spouse, our family, the world, and various organizations. Subjecting my beliefs to scrutiny, I opened my mind to understand possibilities and inquiries better. During my upbringing, I absorbed information without verifying its accuracy, as I was instructed to have blind faith. Unfortunately, this came at a cost I was expected to follow obediently and refrain from asking questions. But when curiosity is stifled, personal growth is stunted, and one's potential is limited.

The underlying, unintended message is that you have the freedom to choose, but somehow, you are persuaded to select what does not truly serve you while being convinced that it does. The answer lies in the creation of fear-based narratives. How can I shatter your security and persuade you to pay me for protection? It is a tactic reminiscent of the Mafia. From the moment I entered this world, I was told I was broken and needed redemption and repair. "Come as you are," they said, "and let us guide you on the right path." Every individual who enters this world is like a blank canvas, ready to absorb and embody whatever is planted in their mind. They become what they think and believe. If you were repeatedly told that you were a king, you would live as royalty. Conversely, if you were repeatedly told you were a misfit, you would live as one not because you want to, but because you believe the narrative. When you hear the phrase "only believe," it is not only for the good but also for the bad; it works both ways.

Why should I perpetuate oppression by acknowledging it, knowing that the more attention I give it, the more I will manifest it for myself and future generations? Instead of succumbing to a victim mentality and waiting for circumstances to change, I recognized the importance of becoming an active change agent. I understood that I needed to shift my perception and deliberately choose the lenses through which I viewed the world. I am not oppressed. I am not a victim; I went through an experience. I do not need to be saved; I need to understand who I am and accept myself as the dominant force in my life.

I realized that to lead others effectively, I must first learn to lead myself. Prioritizing self-care and self-service became essential before extending that care and service to others. Before offering love to others, I recognized the importance of cultivating self-love. Likewise, I understood the significance of fulfilling my needs before giving to others. It was crucial to grant myself forgiveness before extending it to others and accepting myself before embracing others fully. By liberating myself from mental constraints, I could better assist others in their liberation. Active listening became a prerequisite for being heard, and developing patience was necessary before exercising patience with others. To guide others, I had to learn from my struggles and experiences. Ultimately, I understood that profound leadership stems from personal experience and growth.

Effective leadership requires a deep understanding of the experiences and perspectives of those being led. It is only through this understanding that a leader can truly serve the needs of their team. With such understanding, a leader can avoid making assumptions about the needs of their team, which can lead to more good of their team, which can lead to more good than harm. In any organization, the people are the heart of the network. Each individual brings unique challenges and worldviews, and the leader must honor and respect these differences to build a solid and cohesive team.

Effective leadership requires a deep understanding of the experiences and perspectives of those being led.

Empathy is an essential value for achieving greatness. It enables us to understand situations from another person's viewpoint and lead compassionately. A leader who prioritizes self-leadership is highly effective. Their integrity serves as a model to others and attracts positive energy. By loving and embracing myself, I gained valuable insights into my journey and the experiences that shaped me. Through this process, I went from experiencing low energy to high energy and ultimately found a balance.

The language of love is the most potent force in the universe. When I fully embraced and accepted who I am, I attracted a different type of energy and connection into my life. In the past, denying my true identity kept me connected to others who also denied themselves. It was like the saying,

"Misery loves company." Growing up, I often heard the saying, "Show me your friends, and I'll tell you who you are." At first, I was offended by this statement because I felt like I was being judged based on someone else's actions; however, as I matured, I realized that my internal motivation and energy projection attracted certain people and situations into my life. It goes beyond the body.

CHAPTER SIXTEEN:
BEFORE I KNEW ME

There was a time when I perfectly embodied the metaphor of the blind leading the blind. It was like I was hiding from the rain--too afraid to venture out and get wet. Yet, in the great game of life, remaining stagnant and unadventurous puts me at risk even when I try my hardest not to get wet. It never dawns on me to ask, *Why not embrace the rain and allow each drop to touch me?* Let it cascade upon my head, shoulders, skin, and back and trickle down my legs. The answer is based on one's life's unique experiences.

I used to think avoiding my experiences and striving for perfection was the key to happiness. I was constantly at war with myself, using external measures to achieve what I thought I should be instead of embracing who I indeed was. I was so focused on appearing normal that I refused to stand in the rain and feel the raindrops. Looking back, it is amusing how we define "normal." In my culture, there's a common phrase that many people have uttered at some point: "Meh, cannot tell nobody this" (in Jamaican patois). While this phrase may seem like a protective shield, it creates an uncomfortable feeling within oneself.

I pride myself on crossing all the t's and dotting all the i's to protect my heart from getting hurt. It may be easier for some people to shake things off and move on. That was not the case for me. To be honest, I wish it were; it would have saved me a whole lot of unnecessary suffering. It was like I had this feeling that I had to prove my innocence, when it was a cycle I created and got stuck inside. The blind leading blind going around in circles, binding up myself.

People who are hurting often end up hurting others, while those who are emotionally healthy tend to bring healing to those around them. It is not as if someone who is hurting wakes up each day intending to cause harm. No, that is not how it works. Before starting my own family, I was carrying a lot of pain. My way of coping with that pain was to conceal it, never learning how to address and heal from it effectively. I was never taught healthy ways to navigate pain; instead, I would rely on external circumstances to change, believing that it would bring the happiness and fulfillment I sought. Consequently, there seemed to be no reason to explore my inner self if I focused solely on waiting for external changes. When I am hurting, I want others to feel or understand my pain; it is the same when you have a healthy mindset; you want others to feel and understand what you are experiencing.

Ultimately, I realized there was nothing to mend, as I was never damaged or broken. Ironically, despite feeling hurt internally, I was fixated on waiting for external circumstances to resolve everything magically. The truth dawned on me that I was trapped in a relentless cycle of self-imposed suffering. My thoughts held power, governing my emotions and influencing my behavior day in and day out.

This newfound understanding completely transformed my perspective. I realized that I am the architect of my reality, shaping it through the thoughts I choose, the emotions I cultivate, and the actions I take.

I was determined to shield my heart and yearned to be comprehended. I constructed intricate narratives to reinforce my reasons, hoping that my anguish would be validated along with my actions. This habit is perilous since it needs more self-awareness. It is like running on autopilot, similar to a bot programmed to execute a specific task in an algorithm. I used to assume I knew my "why," but my "why" was also conditioned or programmed.

I learned to shoulder numerous responsibilities as a young girl, making me mature beyond my years. My tendency to overthink and avoid pain helped me develop mental strength faster than my peers. In many ways, I became more mature than my mother, often guiding her through essential decisions that would benefit her. Our bond was based on mutual love and care, and it pained me to see her suffering. I hated seeing her cry wildly when she cried for us.

I carried the weight of my mother's happiness on my shoulders, believing that if she were happy, I would be happy, too. My mission was to prevent her from experiencing pain, even if it meant sacrificing my well-being. This mindset was born from my fear of being hurt and my desire to protect her. But in doing so, I failed to see her as a person with her own free will and choices. Instead, I saw her as my mother, and her happiness became my responsibility. I was carrying the burden of her shame and my own without realizing it was not my burden.

My perception at that time needed to be more accurate. After all, I was only a seven-year-old child trying to find the courage and strength to defend my mother. This behavior gradually stripped away my childhood, forcing me to adapt to survive within the family. It became our fight, and I needed to protect my mother at all costs.

The controlling pattern started with my mother, and I took the same attitude in my marriage. The critical point is she is not aware that her actions affected me. Neither of us was aware of its impact on me. It was just another piece of the puzzle of life that we accepted. It felt like running your entire life in a relay race; she passed the baton on to me to carry. I took the baton and ran with it for many years.

I was chaos by definition, attracting more chaos. I lived in the drama triangle of my mind: building more and more images of what I believed others were thinking about my life; blaming people for not being sensitive to my misfortune; and being inconsiderate of others' feelings. I had an attitude that everything revolved around me, but in reality, it did not, but I made it so in my mind.

This way of living opened doors to compromise and set no boundaries for myself or others. I took everything coming to me like a flood, and while drowning, I still used myself as a lifeboat for others. There are two sides to this: selfish and saving myself, or selfless, believing I am saving someone else. As I said in the earlier chapter, I always played the hero in everyone's lives instead of my own. From my own experience in life, I realized no one could save me but myself. I am the only way to a better life for myself. I am the door that opens to more knowledge, understanding, and healing.

Healthy People Heal People

I shared my unhealthy way of life; now, let me share my newness of life. Learning to love me required me to dig deep. I am setting boundaries, building valuable emotional intelligence, learning to please myself first, and practicing healthy habits that teach others how to treat me, not because they want to, but because I will not allow others' actions or words to run my house anymore. My home is where love lives and sits on the seat of my throne daily. I gave up my old mindset and opened myself to a better me.

You may wonder what the catalyst for my shift was. It was I; I was the catalyst for change. I wanted something different than what I had. I was willing to let go of it all. Everything I fought my entire life to keep, I was willing to let go of, and in the end, it turns out it was always mine from the beginning. My family needed me just as much as I needed them. My peace needed me just as much as I needed peace. What I wanted, wanted me back, but the fight was simple. ***I did not know how to receive it.*** Because I was under the impression that I had to do something to get it, I was an expert at pushing people and things away. I did not believe I was worth loving. Therefore, I was pushing away love. I had to go far to find the better me and question everything, which ultimately helped me see myself. I do not need to be loved; I am Love.

When I meet someone, I still cannot wait to tell them about my life, but this time it is about my newness in life. Freedom comes with taking ownership of myself, not waiting to be saved but saving myself from myself. It is the same small-town girl but with a different mindset. I created her the mess of mess, and I created her the gift of life. I am and was always the leader of that little girl. At first, I was leading her from the image I saw outside. Now, I am leading her from within the lighthouse, experiencing the best of both worlds. I am building from home.

I dropped the baton; I decided to pass on a different legacy to my daughter with which to run.

I am a healed woman passing on healing to my future generation. I saved myself and ended up saving a whole generation. Below is my daily affirmation, which I want to share with you, the reader.

> **I am a healer because I chose to heal myself.**
> **There is no failure when your heart pushes you to learn and grow.**
> **What I create brings healing to me and generations to come.**
> **I am thankful for the divine light that shines through me and all.**
> **As we increase in wisdom, understanding, and favor.**

To know oneself is to understand oneself. Understanding myself helps me understand others. It opens the door to compassion, forgiveness, peace, and unconditional love. Everything we need is inside us. The seeker finds, the knocker discovers more, and the questioner gets answers. Look only for what you want. Not what you do not want. Take it from me: anything you look for, you will find; why not look for what you desire? It may seem like it is the foolish way, but in my experience, it ended up being a better way.

God uses foolish things to confuse the wise.

To answer the question, *Is there a cause?* There is a cause for everything, but how far will you go to find it? I heard consistently to go deeper, and every time I went deeper, *This is it*, I thought. Until I go some more and catch an ah-ah moment, I love those moments; it feels like a new level of awareness. You realize everything is not always what it seems, even your perceptions, your imaginations, and why we do what we do consciously and unconsciously.

I learned to mimic what I saw early and tried to rationalize it to fit my most comforting stand. My comfort stand became my bed of roses, and I did not want to leave the known for the unknown. Instead, I blocked my mind's doorway to keep believing the fairytale story I told myself. That I was this princess waiting to be rescued. All along, the rescuer was waiting for me. You would be surprised to know how many things I told myself, and the funny part is I believed my lies. Delusions are more common than we would like to admit.

Going deeper requires honesty. It was the truth that set me free. Not the lies I told myself for so many years. Believing my lies made them real and made them manifest. The truth of who I am is that I Am. Nothing more, nothing less. It means nothing, just another label or camouflage until you go deeper and take the layers off. It is a personal (per SON all) journey to the sacred way of life. When I look in the mirror, I do not look at what I want to see; I look at who I am right before me.

I do not need rules to be changed for me to accept myself. I do not need another person's opinion to be changed for me to accept who I am. I do not need people to act a certain way for me to accept who I am. I do not need a culture to change to accept me for who I am. I do not feel threatened by someone else's belief because that was once me until I met myself. There is no need to convince another because the knower knows.

I lived as many before, but now, I live as one. Holy means one. The same; nothing separates me from me. I am that I am. I did not know I was me before, but now I know. Once you know, you know. Now, there is only one voice in my head. And when I look at the world, I look with my heart, not my eyes. When I speak, I speak as one voice.

Because I am the living word manifesting my belief daily, I must create a plan, be specific, and write down precisely what I want for my future life. As long as I am breathing, I am the living, and the words I speak and believe shape my reality. You, too, are the living word, but your words, not mine. You can use my words or someone else's, but what would it be like if they were yours? Ask yourself that question.

We must ask the right question and save time, as I did on the wrong question. Like, *What's in it for me?* Not what sounds good. Sounding good can be deceptive, requiring much discernment and knowledge. The best advice I can give my daughter is to use her mind to create what she wants without fear. Welcome challenges; they teach you about yourself. Put herself first. Growing up, I heard the scripture put God first. Back then, I thought it was my rituals and devotions. I did not understand then that I must put myself first if God is within me.

Self-love is the first love and the cornerstone upon which all other love is built. Loving myself well means loving my family well, my neighbor well, my coworkers well, my community well, and my country well. Self-care is the action that reflects what the heart is saying. As I unravel my story in this book, you also have a story inside you. Fear is the culprit in robbing people of knowing themselves.

I fall prey to fear not only in my past life but also in my newness of life. The greatest lie I told myself was that if I opened my mind to change my newly discovered viewpoint, I was going against God. This is the most significant sin(*misunderstanding*)I have committed for years, and it is denying oneself. There is no denying that I accept what was and is and aspire to create a new vision for myself and my future.

Life is a gift, and how we live our lives is the gift we give to ourselves and the world. ~ Stephanie Harrington

We give what we are. When we are true to ourselves, there is no need to convince or compel others; we just attract more of ourselves. To truly understand the world, one must understand oneself. There is no fire without a flame except the one that burns within, the burning bush in our soul that wants our attention.

I cannot stress enough that you hold the key to your kingdom. The universe is within; explore your inner landscape with many mansions and acres of land. You are the alchemist, the cultivator of emotions, and the entertainer of thoughts.

I was sharing with my daughter during one of our nightly book readings; the topic was about emotions. I always ask her what she takes away from what she reads. This night, she plunked her head against her headboard and said, "Mom, I don't know how to explain it, but I read it. Can I go to bed now, please?"

I shook my head and said, "Honey, I know you are tired, but I want you to understand the power you have within."

She looked at me with eyes insinuating that mom had left my room and closed the door. I looked at her with eyes and body language that told her, "You must hear this."

I began explaining to her that she is the creator of her emotions. I used analogies that she could understand. I said you are frustrated because you want to go to bed, but Mom insists on lecturing you. I said the feeling you feel; you create it. Mom may be the catalyst or the external influencer, but you are the ultimate creator of that feeling.

She shook her head and exclaimed, "OK, I get it; just go now!"

Then I continued by saying, "Let's talk about boyfriends. They would bring you roses, write you a love letter, and spend time together."

She looked at me because this seemed more interesting. I knew I had gotten her attention, and the mission was to educate.

I explained that when a boy or girl exchanges gifts and spends time together, their emotions are generated within themselves. When they feel the emotion of love, they are experiencing themselves. They were created by themselves from within. The other person's actions may influence them, but the individual ultimately creates their feelings of love. The love they experience results from their belief in the other person's actions. I told her she was the alchemist, the creator of her emotions. This concept also applies to situations where someone says or does something hurtful. Although they may influence her emotions, she ultimately can decide how she responds. Understanding this can help her navigate external influences more effectively, choosing whether to let them affect her. It is a personal choice.

When I shared this with my daughter, she seemed taken aback, as if she had never considered it. I hoped for her to respond with a sense of realization.

She simply replied, "Okay, Mom."

We exchanged a kiss before saying goodnight.

Once you grasp that you are the creator of positive and negative emotions within yourself, you let go of the blame game and focus solely on cultivating the desired emotions. Whether stories, news, or doctrines, any external influence is external. You hold the power to decide what enters your mind. You are a skilled chef crafting a delightful feast for your life. I believe in using your words to shape your reality rather than dwelling on what you do not want, as that is still a form of creation. When cooking, I do not say, "I do not want figs or rotten eggs in my soup." Instead, I actively choose the ingredients I want and add them to my pot. The outcome always aligns with my initial vision.

CHAPTER SEVENTEEN:
AIM ACTIVATING INNER MOTIVATION

Developing mental strength or resilience often involves starting from the endpoint. This method can be complex, mainly when it is a new undertaking. What if you were guaranteed success? How would you approach your life? What changes would you make immediately? What thoughts would run through your head? How would you feel? Pause for a moment and reflect on these statements. Repeat them to yourself and envision how they might manifest in your life.

Activating Inner Motivation (AIM) activates a more profound awareness to help you be intentional when tapping into your willpower as you learn to manage beliefs better. Your beliefs are what take precedence inside your internal landscape. By stimulating your inner drive, you can attain a heightened level of consciousness, enabling you to shape your beliefs and leverage your willpower consciously. This empowers you to shape your reality deliberately. But what I mean by stimulating your inner drive. It means to give your attention to, to observe, to seek to understand, to be curious about.

Let us delve into the concept of willpower. Willpower is an intrinsic quality that originates within us. Our perceptions lay the groundwork for fostering willpower. Willpower is the ability to exercise self-restraint and resist temptations to pursue long-term objectives or choices consistent with one's values and beliefs. It entails exerting conscious effort to overcome automatic or impulsive reactions and instead opt for a more intentional and purposeful approach. Willpower can be enhanced and honed through consistent practice and training.

Based on my experience, willpower is always in action, whether or not I choose to do something. The driving force behind our willpower is the determining factor, much like fuel igniting a flame. In the past, when I created without mindfulness, fear was the fuel that propelled my willpower forward.

Cultivating self-awareness is vital to living a purposeful life. It is connected to living with a sense of intuition. Believing something is true. Your willpower ignites strength and courage to survive. Every day, we are trading our beliefs; that belief may or may not serve us. Our beliefs influence our decision-making, how we view the world and others, and how we connect or communicate with each other. Having a high Pain Tolerance Level (PTL) can enhance the efficiency of your trade. Consider the scenario where your alarm rings at 5 a.m., and you are faced with two options: moving towards or away from motivation.

Moving towards motivation is an inner drive that motivates you to accomplish tasks with passion and determination. It does not rely on any external factors to persuade you to act. Moving away from motivation is driven by fear, making you feel like you have no choice but to take action. When your alarm goes off, you might postpone getting out of bed for another twenty minutes, or you may need to persuade yourself to do something. It all comes down to your emotional pain tolerance level, which determines your ability to bear discomfort and helps you make better decisions. Only one thing can facilitate the creation or operation of a flow state. When I am in a flow state, time stands still, I feel completely immersed in what I am doing, and creativity comes naturally. I end up doing what I love and loving what I do. This state is achieved through internal motivation. Not being internally motivated can keep you trapped in a life you wish to escape, settling for something you do not truly desire.

My grandmother had a saying that still holds today: "Where there is a will, there is a way." Willpower is a powerful force that can generate opportunities, forge connections, and network, all the qualities necessary for building a successful business. Without willpower, one is left in the dark, merely hoping and wishing for things to happen.

By Activating your Inner Motivation, you can effectively identify and address your struggles and determine from which end of the spectrum you are operating. Clarity is a critical component integral to Activating Inner Motivation (AIM). In the following discussion, we will delve deeper into this concept.

The three primary keys to Activating Inner Motivation (AIM) are Self-awareness, Intentionality, and Self-Management. Consider your current circumstances, whether they are feeling stuck, unfulfilled, lacking, dealing with fear, relationship issues, or work-related challenges. Imagine your best self--living your best life, achieving your career and relationship goals, and more.

The first key to Activating Inner Motivation (AIM) is **Self-awareness,** which involves being mindful of your thoughts, emotions, and beliefs. Your thoughts may include your self-talk and imagination, while your emotions may range from fear, worry, loneliness, shame, and loss to unhappiness. Your beliefs about your current situation are not what you want them to be but what they are when you consider them. In reality, what you are doing reflects your current state of mind. This reflection provides the clarity you need to move forward and make progress.

To initiate the process of AIM, begin by asking yourself the fundamental question: **"Is my current situation within my control?"** To answer this question, consider whether the issue is external, such as another person, a boss, a friend, or a family member. If it is something beyond your control, then the answer is *no*. On the other hand, if it is an internal issue, such as a belief, emotion, perception, or physical or emotional state, then the answer is *yes*.

Utilizing this fundamental will shift your attention away from the problem and toward finding a solution. By doing so, you can develop a stronger connection with yourself and clarify what motivates you internally or externally.

The second key is being **Intentional.** Exploring your willpower can enhance your ability to create and develop what you desire. Your attention is a powerful force that fuels your creations, requiring direction and guidance. Whether we acknowledge it or not, our attention shapes our daily experiences. Therefore, why not consciously create what we truly want for ourselves by focusing our attention intentionally?

The second key helps us to let go of the **question** and immerse our **attention** in the **answer.**

Based on your answer from the first key, you should have a **yes or no, asking if your current situation is within your control.** If it is a:

YES - How can I learn to change it?

NO - How can I learn to let it go?

I want to clarify that I am not suggesting you should simply "change" or "let go" of a problem without further consideration. If it were that easy, you would have already done it. Instead, the purpose is to learn to take responsibility for your life. In the past, when I heard the phrase "take responsibility," I felt offended. I believed others judged me as lazy, immature, or ignorant. Let me explain what taking responsibility truly means.

You have the right to choose how you respond to life. You can be a conscious or unconscious participant in your own experiences. Being responsible means acknowledging that your response to a situation is within your control. You can make a choice based on your knowledge and understanding of the situation or challenge at hand.

RESPONSE*ABLE

Sometimes, you may need help responding to a situation, but seeking assistance is still possible. In my own experience, I used to view asking for help as a sign of weakness, which ultimately became a stumbling block. I was quick to complain but hesitant to ask for help as it felt like admitting failure. This was particularly challenging when I started as a novice trader and experienced many losses. I felt like a failure and tried to avoid that feeling at all costs. I would blame external factors such as the market, faulty software, or rigged trading platforms rather than accept responsibility for my mistakes.

The same goes for our beliefs. Our beliefs can hold us back if we cling to them despite their ineffectiveness. As Albert Einstein famously noted, repeating the same thing daily and hoping for a different outcome is a sign of insanity. I can relate to this behavior as I used to make excuses such as "I do not have enough money," "That's not for me," or "What if I cannot pay my bills," which prevented me from taking responsibility for my life and making positive changes.

Although it may seem challenging, letting go of these limiting beliefs is possible. When my husband and I sold our house and business and pursued our dreams, we received a significant return on our investment due to the high market value. Despite having enough funds to live stress-free for at least three years, I worried about how long the money would last and contemplated numerous "what if" scenarios. In essence, my attention was consumed by worry and fear.

Although our financial situation had drastically changed, my mindset remained the same. Despite my newfound financial stability, I still had a scarcity mentality instead of an abundance mentality, and my focus stayed the same. I realized I needed to reframe and reprogram my brain intentionally towards an abundance mindset. This task was challenging, as I tend to question everything and seek more profound meaning, sometimes leading to unnecessary complications. I accepted this trait, however, as a blessing and a curse, learning to use it effectively.

Upon reflection, I recognized that my attention was still governed by fear rooted deeply in worry. I challenged myself to confront everything that scared me head-on to break this mindset. I called this approach "reckless self-love," which may sound impulsive to some but allowed me to face and overcome my fears. Only some people are comfortable taking such bold steps; some may require help.

Help may come in the form of a life coach, counselor, business coach, trainer, healthy habit plan, course, program, therapist, etc. It is not a friend you tell your problem to get sympathy; they do not know how to help you, especially, if they have the same mindset as you. From my experience, you would be told what they would do if it were them, and truthfully, they do not know what they would do if faced with your specific situation. I learned early that people like to talk, and we like to comfort each other, mainly if their pain affects us. I know because I sit in that seat at times. But you **do**

not know what you can endure until you have endured yourself. It is best to talk to someone who already has had experience in the area you need help with; experience is gold because they are challenged by feelings of the other's infirmity or unrest. Not only were they touched by it, they overcame it.

Be open to the possibility that you may not have all the answers. You may need to follow someone else's blueprint until you can create your own. With Intentionality, we aim to tap into our willpower and be more purposeful with our thoughts, emotions, and actions.

The third essential element is **Self-Management**.

You are taking inspired action and prioritizing self-improvement. You become the intentional "DOER" in your life. As you embark on your journey towards a healthier lifestyle and personal growth, you must acknowledge the stages of awareness and competency you may encounter. The following chart can be a helpful guide:

Stage 1: Unconscious Incompetence	At this stage, you may not know how your thoughts, emotions, and beliefs impact your life. You may not realize that you can shape your reality and create a more fulfilling life.
Stage 2: Conscious Incompetence	In this stage, you realize you are the creator of your reality. You understand that your thoughts, emotions, and beliefs are powerful tools that can help or hinder your personal growth. You become aware of areas in which you need to improve.
Stage 3: Conscious Competence	At this stage, you are actively taking steps to retrain your brain and adopt more purposeful thoughts, emotions, and beliefs. You are

	committed to personal growth and recognize that making lasting changes takes effort and practice.
Stage 4: Unconscious Competence	In this final stage, you have mastered your new healthy habits and ways of thinking. You have integrated them into your daily life; they come naturally and effortlessly to you. You are the "DOER," and your new habits are a part of who you are.

The ultimate goal is to reach unconscious competence, where you are no longer consciously trying to improve but simply living your best life. Remember, life is meant to be embraced, not just endured, so keep striving towards personal growth and living your best life.

You will need tools, and as I said in earlier chapters, you cannot build a house without tools. Tools involve dedicating more time to personal practices such as meditation, breathing exercises, prayer, affirmations, self-reflection, and, most importantly, alone time.

Self-management also entails making peace with your past, confronting your fears truthfully, and acknowledging pain while working towards forgiveness. Working out my forgiveness is like the ghost of the past, revisiting with a feeling and an idea. Sometimes, it may take an hour or less for me to realize I am not that person anymore. Those thoughts are not my own in this instance, and I feel them, examine them, ask myself the tricky questions, and be honest with myself as to why I had entertained those emotions and feelings before. Then, the best part is forgiving myself with compassion and love.

Reading books in areas where you need healing can be an effective tool for self-development. Pursuing further education or attending workshops can also be beneficial in this regard. It is, however, through learning and gaining knowledge, that your change in belief and acceptance facilitates the healing process.

The concept of **Activating Inner Motivation** (AIM) is a powerful tool for breaking free from the victim mentality syndrome.

For most of my life, I blamed others for my problems and sought revenge, using various excuses to justify my self-destructive behavior. I lacked self-discipline and control, and my emotions would run wild, causing chaos and turmoil. My "pity me" and condemning self-talk were the pack's leaders.

I was convinced that someone else was responsible for my emotional pain, and I would often say things like, "You do not know how you made me feel." This response was, of course, to manipulate others or convince myself of my victimhood. This phrase is prevalent and easy to multiply, especially in my environment growing up.

I eventually realized that I alone am responsible for my feelings and emotions. By giving someone else the power to control my happiness or freedom, I essentially imprisoned myself and surrendered the key to my emotional well-being. This realization was a turning point for me, and I began to take ownership of my thoughts and emotions, freeing myself from the grip of the victim mentality and taking control of my own life.

Self-management is actively working on your "Action Plan." Knowledge is nothing with exercising what you have learned, which is the very definition of wisdom. Breaking free from thinking "I should" to "being" will take time. You are reducing your debt to yourself and increasing your wealth to a happier, healthier you. You are now the giver in your life, which ultimately flows out to others.

As a natural giver who finds joy in seeing others happy, there is a risk of becoming vulnerable and quickly taken advantage of. It is not that the people taking advantage of you are doing it deliberately; instead, they are simply utilizing what they can from you to make their lives easier or more comfortable. That is why you must establish healthy boundaries and know when to say *no*, even if it may be difficult for you as a compassionate and giving person. While generosity and kindness are admirable traits, they can also become weaknesses if overused. You may feel drained and resentful, with nothing left to give, and potentially isolate yourself.

There is an argument that giving without expecting anything in return is the ultimate form of generosity. While this may be true, it is essential to remember that when you give, you should rationalize the potential loss to yourself and not allow it to drain your self-worth. Setting boundaries and practicing self-care is crucial to maintaining a healthy balance between giving to others and caring for yourself. Remember, being kind and compassionate to others starts with being kind and compassionate to yourself.

CHAPTER EIGHTEEN:
THE PLACE PREPARED FOR ME

I am fighting with myself when I try to control the outcome. Life is very unpredictable, and sometimes the result may not always work out the exact way you hope for.

Sometimes, what I want may be different from what I need. I always want what seems safer and more comfortable, but what I need may require stretching and giving more of myself. This was my hardest life lesson. It was not just being open to the unexpected, going with the flow, and allowing myself to trust. No, it is going against a thought or emotion I had before, especially when I always took the defensive stand. The belief that I wanted to protect my heart is not seen with the naked eye. It is a feeling connected to a narrative that supports itself and gears your attention to seek out what seems like an attack or pointing a finger. Self-preservation comes naturally over self-sacrifice since that is my preferred mental cycle.

I was tired of believing my own lies that I was being victimized.

I did anything to prevent mental pain and suffering; whatever I had to tell myself, I did it to feel better. But I had an underdeveloped emotional state of mind. I was tired of believing my own lies that I was being victimized. I was afraid of the unknown. I was afraid of what I had never experienced or believed existed.

So, Was I Fighting a Feeling or Fighting Myself?

It turns out I was fighting a feeling. I realized that my entire life on earth was an experience; it was not a death sentence. All the challenges were tools to mold and make me into the woman I am becoming. So, instead of continuing to play defense, I pivoted to offense, recognizing that all challenges are opportunities to grow, and that I needed to fight for myself by going against breaking down all the barriers, walls, and security systems I had created. I asked, "If I do not fight for myself, who will?" I believe everyone must ask themselves this question and then stop and listen with an open mind and unbiased heart.

Fighting for myself entails a change in my perspective and a new foundation. What I create impacts the lives around me, especially my daughter, and how I connect and communicate with people. It is like a snowball effect; a transforming life transforms lives. I fought for myself, my mother, sister, friend, cousin, grandmother, daughter, and every woman and girl battling generational bondage.

I fought to CreateHER, BuildHER, and LeadHer.

God made us all, but the woman I shared with you in this book, I CreateHER. The things I did daily builtHER. My next step, believe it or not, was every step I took leadingHER. Today, I rest in the faith to consciously createHER, the woman I am proud of. I do the things daily that will buildHER and always remember to take the next best step because my next step, your next best step, will leadHER. The Creator of the Universe is inside me and in everything around us. When you speak, your words will not come back void but accomplish whatever they are set to do. I am creating what I say and what I couple with an emotion. God is creating through me.

I created those beliefs; however, they were influenced by outside sources or personal experience. I had to learn to take another look, step back, and see what is not apparent but is noticeable. But guess what? I can recreate new beliefs and create a better daily narrative. Because the word of my mouth and the meditation of my heart will be accepted and not come back void. I healed my broken heart and taught myself to love again. To love me, to give myself compassion and forgiveness. To not see myself as what someone else's narrative is.

I did not realize, until years after coming to terms with my creation, that I hated myself. I felt like an imposter in my skin, and I affirmed it by repeating and believing the narrative of brokenness, oppression, and victimhood. It is like taking on a role in a movie, but getting lost in the role and forgetting who you are in the first place. I played the role of a mother, a wife, a friend, and an abiding citizen of society, but never the dominant force in my life. I never controlled my mind and beliefs and developed my emotional intelligence. How could I? I was a product of my environment, but now I have no excuse.

I am the lighthouse. The light is never outside. It is inside each human being. I can leave my lights on or turn them off. Whether we turn the light off or on affects our environment, especially home life. Home is where love lives and gives. Home is your internal landscape.

You never know who you will inspire with your story. There is always a ship at sea needing direction. It may not be for everyone, but if it is only for one ship, that one ship may carry millions on board. I bear my heart and soul in this book not to show how difficult my journey was, for we all have experienced challenges--some more difficult than others--but I intend to provide another lens to give the open-minded woman or man another perspective. To share my newfound freedom, the burden of light.

I have nothing to prove to others, but to myself that I was worth dying for. Dying to the "what ifs," "what they thinks," "judgments," and "others' opinions"--the lies I told myself, the beliefs I created. The cross to bear is not something I only wear around my neck; it is going against everything you have been sold your entire life and choosing differently. It is standing up for what you believe in. It is self-sacrifice, not self-preservation. It is looking within for answers when you are told to look outside. It is getting a better understanding rather than running with what sounds good, but you never actually do your research.

To leave the ninety-nine and go after the one is to be separated from the masses, sit alone, and be open to learning, growing, and expanding while the ninety-nine entertain each other.

The road to success is lonely. There are so many distractions that we cannot get our attention off ourselves. I, too, am not immune to it. The fight was always for "my attention." What you give your attention to also takes your time and money. My mind is my most prized possession, my birthright. It will grow anything that is planted in it. I am the farmer planting what I want to reap, not what is imposed on me. *As a child, I did not know how to protect my land, but now I am an adult and claim full ownership of my REAL estate. This step of faith gave me the courage to write about my mess, turn my mess into a message, and take my mess higher. My mess AGED gave me experience and added more color to my life.*

I passionately write about this because this was my mental prison for years. I lived most of my life waiting and preparing to go live somewhere else when I came to this earth to live *this* experience. I was not present because my mind was always on the afterlife. I lived very fearfully and ignorant of what love looks and feels like. I am not blaming anyone because that would mean I am doing the same thing again by laying my life in someone else's hands. I now live unapologetically and authentically myself--very loud, and I need no validation to be *me*.

There is no denying the hand I was given; I must take ownership of who and where I am now. I do not need to know what I did not know, but I must know who I am and never deny myself being me. It was time for me to heal her and create her future.

When you submit to an experience and rise with much understanding, there is much to gain. All along, I thought I was fighting the feeling of fear, shame, and labels. I thought I was fighting others' opinions of me. I thought I was fighting a broken system. I thought I was fighting religion. I thought I was fighting cultural differences. I thought I was fighting traditions. I thought I was fighting societal norms, and the list goes on. But in reality, whose report did I believe? "It was my report." I was fighting MYSELF!

Our ancient text states, **"It is done unto you as you believe."**

I believed in the shame. I believed in the fear. I believed in the negative self-talk. I affirmed the oppression. I affirmed the victimhood mentality. I believed in the distorted images I created of myself. Getting understanding releases you from one particular experience to the next and also activates compassion and empathy for others.

I am fascinated by the captivating tale of the lotus flower. Despite its humble origins in muddy and murky waters, it emerges as the epitome of beauty, triumphing over every obstacle. Symbolizing rebirth and the promise of new beginnings, it represents a transformation from what once was to what is. As a young girl, I vividly recall sketching these aquatic blooms, unsure of the origin of my inspiration. Nevertheless, I distinctly remember the tranquility that washed over me as I dedicated my time to delicately illustrate each petal. It was as if time stood still, allowing me to immerse myself in the art entirely.

The lotus is a powerful symbol, reflecting the stages of growth in my own life. Each petal represents a different phase, much like the various stages of my personal development. It all began in the depths of the water, reminiscent of the time spent within my mother's womb, surrounded by darkness and unaware of my true potential. My focus was primarily external during this period, and self-imposed suffering hindered my exploration of the inner realm.

Similar to how a baby gradually develops, our minds also require time to mature, with our environment playing a significant role in shaping our awareness and understanding. But as I emerged from the depths and glimpsed the light above the water's surface, a newfound energy propelled me to reach upward. I directed my attention toward the nourishing light, which illuminated my beauty, unveiled my vibrant colors, and granted me the gift of sight.

This light represents knowledge, awareness, love, acceptance, and freedom. It signifies the illumination of my path, guiding me toward a life filled with wisdom, compassion, and self-discovery. Like the lotus, I have blossomed, transcending the limitations of my past and embracing the transformative power of enlightenment.

CHAPTER NINETEEN:
TURN THE LIGHT ON!

She is bright,
She is radiant,
She is glow,

She rises like the sun,
She gives light to the world,
She is the circle of life,

She is full of colors,
She sparkles and shines,
She glitters like gold.

She is you. She is me.
She did not know she was a Creator.

Embracing oneself fully and without denial is the gateway to enlightenment. It entails a profound acceptance of who you are, free from shame or unworthiness. When this understanding takes root within, a fire ignites an intense passion that fuels your journey forward. It is a transformative experience where you release the grip on the past and wholeheartedly embrace the present moment.

The words you read earlier reflected my past, a narrative of what once was. But now, with intention and purpose, I have crafted a new story of living with a clear sense of direction and meaning. It was a conscious choice to reshape my reality. I am no longer defined by what was but empowered by what is and will be.

Living intentionally paves the way for a new era of prosperity for oneself and the world. It involves embracing every opportunity that comes your way and fearlessly sharing your unique light with others. You catalyze positive change and transformation by consciously directing your actions and choices. Your presence radiates a powerful energy that uplifts and inspires those around you. With unwavering confidence and a commitment to making a difference, you become a beacon of inspiration for a brighter future.

Within you resides the light, for you embody the divine. You are the church, a vessel where the radiant light of love dwells and emanates. By prioritizing your well-being and nurturing the light within, you align yourself with the essence of love itself. When you honor and nurture yourself, everything else naturally falls into place. You become a magnet for blessings, abundance, and joy as the light within you expands and touches every aspect of your life. With each step you take, you embody the power of love and radiate its transformative energy to the world around you.

To shine is to elevate and enrich one's existence, infusing it with purpose and significance. It is to embrace an inner radiance that emanates outwardly. Living from the inside out entails a deep understanding of one's essence, allowing it to guide and shape our authentic expression. It is a graceful and opulent dance, evoking a sense of allure and sensuality akin to delicate pearls adorning the neck. When we shine, we illuminate our path with beauty and meaning, inspiring others to embrace their inner light and live with purposeful elegance.

The inherent treasures within cannot be purchased, for salvation is not a transaction but a gift freely bestowed upon us by us. Our choices shape our path, and we embrace the abundance already within us. Let me acquaint you with your true self, your divine essence. The divine within me acknowledges and honors the divine within me, recognizing the unity that binds us as one.

For countless years, I wandered through the wilderness, heeding the voices of those who themselves denied their true essence. Driven by the fear of persecution, they concealed their authentic selves. However, my readers, refuse to be confined within the boundaries of someone else's perception. I would rather face persecution for being true to myself than be captive to another's limited understanding.

I permitted myself to thrive. Many people pursue consistent and profitable experiences as their ultimate goal. With unwavering dedication and persistent effort, anything can be achieved. Success is not a gift bestowed upon a fortunate few but rather the result of continuous self-work and personal development.

Flip the switch by manifesting your desires through the transformation of your mindset.

It is a common saying that the lion is not the giant creature in the animal kingdom, yet it attains its desires through its attitude. To draw in what you desire, you must boldly assert it. Set your intention and feel the sensation of already achieving what you want.

Darkness to light can be as simple as a mindset shift or increased knowledge and understanding. Every experience I've had holds no regrets, as it has provided me with a newfound purpose and taught me the importance of valuing and nurturing my present state of being. Reflecting on things now, I can confidently say this, although I may not have been able to acknowledge such while I was in the midst of the experiences. I realized that mere survival is not enough; it is a deceptive illusion that keeps you hidden and stagnant. Actual progress and fulfillment come from having a clear sense of purpose, which propels you forward and amplifies your creativity. If you take a closer look, you'll notice that the ones who often face the most criticism are the ones who dare to be creative. These individuals go against the grain and do things differently, even when it may not align with the perceived norms. If something bothers you deeply or drives you to frustration, it could be a sign from your inner self urging you to take action. It may be an invitation to create something of value that can replace or enhance what already exists. As we continually evolve and grow, so does our creativity. Through these internal prompts, we can tap into our innovative spirit and contribute to the world around us. Embrace these inner stirrings as an opportunity to positively impact and bring forth new and valuable creations.

You will become the switch to turn the light on in that specific situation. The light of knowledge or understanding. The light of sharing your own life experiences. The light of mastering yourself. The light of self-sacrifice. The light of independent thinking. The light of gratitude. The light of releasing yourself from mental slavery. The light of letting go of oppression and breaking free from the victim mentality. My journey of wanting more of myself required me to spend quality time alone, go deeper, and ask the right questions. The risk of being considered different is worth the journey. It takes courage to do your due diligence and to go against the norm.

I was unaware of my role as a creator and that I alone held the power to save myself. I had to embark on a journey of self-discovery, learning to enhance my trust, broaden my perspective, and elevate my worth.

**Choose the direction your heart pushes you
to learn and grow.**

**Not being afraid to fail is part of your alignment.
It is one of the best ways to get into position.**

Are you ready for a change? To liberate yourself from generational traumas and from being a pawn of mass media's influence? Are you open to recognizing that limitations and opportunities exist and that you alone possess the power to determine what constrains you? You are only limited by your thoughts and what you believe. You can learn to avoid getting attached to an outcome because life is not about certainty. This may be more challenging than it sounds, especially, if like me, you desired certainty all the time as I did in the first half of my life. I had to learn to let go of what I thought I knew and embrace a probabilistic viewpoint.

Prob comes from the Latin origin meaning "prove." A probabilistic viewpoint, or probability, requires time to examine the evidence without attachment to the outcome. I see this as an experiment by doing something repeatedly or remaining consistent to prove or provide the data you need to conclude. We may want to reach a goal by practicing something new, incorporating a plan, and executing that plan--not one try and giving up, or two tries and giving up, but doing it repeatedly until the evidence appears profitable or not profitable.

Reconstruct your mindset by incorporating new codes into your life. You can enhance the quality of your existence through affirmations and mindful self-talk. This, in turn, enriches your overall well-being, propelling you toward incredible wealth, health, and prosperity. The more you affirm fulfillment, the more you feel fulfilled. The more you affirm peace and safety in your life, the more you feel peace and safety. What you affirm, you attract. The more you affirm rich relationships, the more loyal friends appear in your life. The more you affirm wealth, the more business opportunities appear. To affirm, you repeat what you believe you already have. Your affirmations do not sound like "I want" or "I desire." Instead, say, "I have." You will realize the more you say you want something, the more you affirm that you do not have it. When you affirm you *have*, somehow, what you affirm makes its way to you as you believed it to be.

Intentional living can pave the way for a new generation of abundance. Embrace every opportunity that comes your way, fearlessly radiating the light wherever you may venture. Everyone is operating from their level of understanding. It is not your fault someone else will not take the time to get to know themselves and grow their mind. Do not dim your light because someone else cannot find their switch or is too scared to turn theirs on. Instead, shine so they will see.

Do not dim your light because someone else cannot find their switch or is too scared to turn theirs on. Instead, shine so they will see.

Dig all the clutter, guilt, shame, and busyness out of your mind. Stop being so hard on yourself. Remember, you are the only way to your mind and heart, and when you beat yourself down, believe it is you, not someone else or a system. It is all in what we tell ourselves. It starts in the internal mirror and then reflects to the external. We can hold our minds captive, not realizing it was coding gone wrong. Decide to re-code and write yourself a new program, a new code. You can start as simply as writing yourself an intimate letter. This was my love letter.

To: The girl that never gave up.

I am thankful for your constant desire to want more of yourself. There is no failure when your heart pushes you to learn and grow. You did your best with what you were given; I am very grateful. No more reflecting on past traumas; it did not kill you, only showed you how powerful you are. You were always the one. The one that is enough, enough to let go of all guilt, enough to love again, enough to create the woman you are proud of. You were never lost or neglected or broken. You had a demanding experience. Divine order continues to govern your life. Now, I permit you to let go of the image you have created of your past self and see nothing but the truth. Let the threat of lack and insufficient validation fade from you. You are enriched with an open mind and heart to receive good health and wealth.

See nothing but abundance in what you create, build, and support because it adds much value to many lives worldwide. You are like the flower that opens up in the mornings; you bring healing warmth and beauty. Grow the garden you want to harvest hope from. Cultivate good thoughts and remain positive. Look only for the good in yourself and others. You will always find what you are looking for. Remember, your mind is that garden, and it will grow anything you plant in it. You are the only way to your heart and your mind. You are the gatekeeper, the watcher, the seer, and the observer. Work from the heart, work from home. Home is where love lives. You are home. You are where love gives. Tell them about home. Thank you for never giving up on yourself.

Everything operates according to divine order; nothing is out of place or falling apart.

Repeat this attitude with boldness and confidence, understanding that you are the conscious leader in your mind and it is time to leadHER. Life is what we make of it. We are the artist, the chef, and the gardener. Be ready to take your mess higher and raise your attitude above the line.

The unknown can be daunting.

The uncertainty of what lies ahead can instill a sense of dread. It becomes challenging to maintain consistency and productivity amidst this uncertainty. Nonetheless, setting goals and striving to achieve them is commendable and courageous. Sometimes, even after reaching a goal, the feeling of fulfillment eludes us, leading us to set another goal in search of satisfaction.

To help myself better comprehend the meaning of my life, I posed a crucial question: *What does my life mean to me?* While there are countless ways to answer this question, every individual's journey is unique. The answer lies in self-reflection, understanding nature, and with no attachment to anything. This is how we can conclude our existence on this earth. My life meant growth and expansion of my mind, creating experiences that foster constantly changing and learning opportunities.

Engaging in activities like listening to high-frequency music can help shift our energy. Additionally, exercise is a powerful form of self-care, awakening the healing mechanisms within our bodies and putting them to work for our benefit. Incorporating meditation and prayer can help us realign and refocus our minds and attention. They provide an opportunity to balance and center our focus amidst the chaos of the unknown. Expressing gratitude is an excellent way to flood our bodies with positive intentions and emotions, fostering a sense of well-being and appreciation. The unknown allows us to discover unexplored aspects of ourselves and our capabilities.

CHAPTER TWENTY:

HIS CHAPTER

I am sure most people want to know why someone would rob a bank and put their family through the challenges that followed that decision. I still do not have a clear reason as to why I went into that Bank of America right as they opened, walked to the teller and casually passed a note with my demands for the money in the drawer. At this point in my life, I truly believed I was the cause of all my family's heartaches and issues. From the age of eighteen until the moment I walked into that bank, I struggled with drug addiction. When I met Stephanie, something inside me just knew she was going to be my wife. She was everything I was not: honest, sweet, beautiful, God-fearing, hardworking, an all-around responsible adult.

Anyone who has ever been in love knows that the beginning stages of it is like a high in itself. This natural high replaced my desire to look for a high in another substance, so during my courting of Stephanie I was sober and able to pull myself together quite well. I truly believed I had finally won my battle with addiction and was going to live happily ever after. Thinking back on this just reminds me of how immature and naive I was.

We dated for a year, then got married, and nine months later came our beautiful little girl. It was not long after that when all the newness of these things started to wear off and I found myself reverting to my old behaviors.

There are no quick fixes or shortcuts in life; bandages are only temporary. Before I knew it, I was in full-blown addiction, bringing all the trauma into my family's life that comes with that. My addiction ultimately caused us to have to separate, and I found myself living on my mother's couch while my girls were living at my father in-law's house. My family was completely torn apart, and no matter how much I tried, I just could not break free from the grip of my addiction.

Many times, I found myself thinking about ending my life, not just thinking about it, but planning it. I knew something drastic had to happen in my life for there to be a change, or I needed to remove myself from the lives of the people I loved the most because I was the main source of their pain.

So, that's the catalyst for the decision we'll say, but then, "Why a bank?" you might ask.

I grew up in Boston, not Beacon Hill or the North Shore type of Boston. I am talking public housing: the Section 8, Charlestown, Southie, Somerville, Dorchester type of Boston. I did not know any doctors or lawyers on a first name basis unless I was being treated or defended by one. Who I did know very well were wise guys, drug dealers, drug addicts, robbers, and bank robbers. In my neighborhood, bank robbers were the most respected and admired. I am no psychologist or human behavioral specialist, but it is pretty safe to say that your surroundings when growing up become like computer code programmed in you and on your perception of life. I am in no way making excuses for my actions or believe in any way they were justified; I am also just trying to make sense of why anyone does the crazy stuff they do. We have all done stuff that people around us have judged us for, but inside we felt there was a legitimate excuse for doing that particular thing. I think a lot of what we do is just autopilot and our subconscious acting out the programming embedded in our psyche.

I used to see guys who were a complete mess go to prison for a few years and come out looking brand new, healthy, in shape, clear-headed and motivated. All the things I wanted in life but just could not do it on my own. I cannot say for sure if this were my exact plan. Let's be honest: I was not in my right mind and had not been for quite some time, but ultimately, it was the best thing that could have happened to me at that time, call it divine intervention, if you will.

I knew I left my family in a tough situation, but I had already done that way before I ever stepped foot in that bank. I remember when the FBI got me, and I was in the bank of the blacked-out SUV. The agent, who moments earlier had a gun to the back of my head while I was being cuffed, looked back at me right in the eye in such a way—the way a loving father look at his son--and said, "It's all over son. You're gonna get the help you need finally."

To this day, I truly believe that was not him speaking to me it was (whatever you wanna call it, *The Universe, Higher-self, Yahweh, etc.,* I am gonna go with) God speaking through him.

For the next few years, I dedicated myself to getting in the best shape of my life, not only physically, but mentally, as well. I was on a mission to get home as fast as I could and finally be the father and husband I always wanted to be. I wish I could say it was as easy as it sounds, but like I said at the beginning, there are no quick fixes or shortcuts in life. It was time to finally heal the wounds without the bandages.

CHAPTER TWENTY-ONE:
WHAT IT TOOK? IT TOOK TIME

My husband served his time in prison for the crime he committed. I served my time in my mental prison for lack of knowledge and understanding. Both journeys took time and gave us hardcore experience, as well as, a new and enlightened perspective on life. Throughout our journey, we experienced faith, hope, and love, but love was and is the greatest of all three.

Love helped me to let go of what was and embrace what is. Love was patient with me. Love was kind to me even when I continued to beat myself up. Self-acceptance created more space for my self-healing. Love taught me to trust. Trusting first in myself and letting go of the outcome. Keeping myself tied to the outcome only magnifies the "what if" on my mind daily. At the beginning of my journey, I was so fixated on my shame, hardship, and survival that I never gave myself the chance of a probabilistic outcome.

Instead, I would channel all my energy and mind builders to assume the worst outcome—all driven by fear. Older folks have a saying, "It's only a matter of time." Today, I am saying it took time. Time is our friend. Time gave me data from my experiences. I used the time to observe my patterns and analyze the talking heads in my mind. I took time to reflect and focus on what matters most to me. What is the meaning behind what I put my energy into? Time reveals my true intentions, the motives behind my actions, and my thought patterns. We needed time to understand ourselves.

Time creates opportunities for us to grow. Time is like a mirror reflecting the past, present, and future. The mirror of time showed us who we were, what we believed ourselves to be, and who we could become. Sometimes, all we need is time. The misconception is that sometimes, we believe we are running out of time. If you believe this statement just like I did, I will tell you to return in time. Be present and ask yourself what you need to learn now because you are precisely where you need to be.

Time. It taught me that happy people create happy marriages. Happy people create happy lives. Happy people are creative. Happy people do things that contribute to their happiness. The mirror of time showed me that I was not happy with myself. I was not happy with my choices. I was not happy with what I created for myself. Time healed my wounds and changed my life by allowing me space to accept that only I have the power to recreate my perception of my life. Time showed me who I am and my capabilities and capacity. Time exposed me to different experiences on my journey from which I was able to learn.

I love, honor, and accept myself as I am. Because I accept myself, I understand better how to accept others. Time secured the gift within me until I was ready to activate it. Self-activation took courage to free myself from my self-limiting beliefs. I encourage you, reader, to say to yourself:

I love your smile, I love your skin, I love your eyes, I love your nose, I love your hair. I love your toes; I love your ankle. I love your hands, I love your belly, I love your back from toes to the crown of my head.

Compliment your weaknesses and strengths. Acknowledge everything you can think of about yourself with love, compassion, and acceptance. Seek understanding always. Wrap your arms around yourself and feel the warm embrace.

Repeat this practice as often as possible, reigniting the feeling throughout your body and signaling to your brain that this is your norm. Become the energy shifter within your body, actively creating a better feeling with your image of yourself. Kids hear the phrase, "It starts at home." It is the same with us. It starts with us. We are home. We are where love lives and love gives.

Growth may feel and look different for everyone. Our journey is laced with different stages upon which we can actively decide to immerse ourselves-- whether a learning experience or taking on a challenge. It is all in our perspective and coping mechanisms. Nevertheless, change is happening in and around us; we should focus more on the changes *inside* than outside.

I find immense delight in witnessing my personal growth as I overcome my previously immature mindset and humble myself to be open to learning. Free from the constraints of my ego and self-criticism, I relinquish the pride of being a resilient black woman and instead embrace a sense of empowerment and happiness. I actively seek opportunities to broaden my horizons and nurture my personal development.

"Learn to Focus" became my motto: simple but impactful words. Trying to stay focused was not enough; I needed to learn to stay focused. Understanding that I do not have all the answers was vital to finding solutions. Even though I believe everything is already inside me, I may not know how to activate the gift within. I had to learn to focus on mental freedom, health, wellness, wealth, and building prosperous relationships. The value is in the learning: the prices you are willing to pay and the risks you are willing to take. It is the little things we do daily with our time and attention.

Believing you deserve something, writing it down, and even speaking it out loud is just the beginning. How do you stay the course after you set sail? Every morning, I remind myself to stay on the course using the tools I have created. Everything in the box below represents me. It is essential that I not only set goals but also be present and focus on learning rather than crossing off another achievement.

Everything in the box below represents what I have control over. This keeps me focused on learning about my health, finances, relationships, and fun time. This may only be for some, but finding balance is what works for me. All the different areas in the four triangles need your time and attention. And you decide what you need from each triangle.

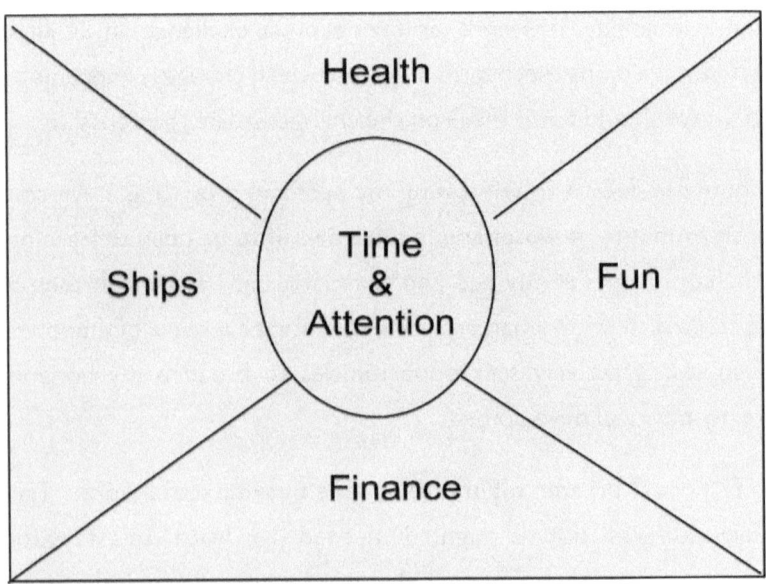

The HEALTH of My Mind, Body, and Spirit

A healthy mind makes better choices. A healthy body is more energized, and a healthy spirit person is more in tune and present. When we dissect the word Healthy, we are left with Heal "THY," which exemplifies my responsibility to have a Healthy Mind, Body, and Spirit. I heal my mind by opening up to learning new things, unlearning some things, and learning how to think by limiting thoughts that drain my energy. I would limit myself to five minutes on a negative thought, then let it go. I train myself to think the thoughts I want. But this is only because I was an overthinker and experienced the negative impact of what I did not want.

Some examples of what I use to help transform my mind are reading books about healthy mindsets, reflecting on what thoughts were romping through my mind all day, and repeating affirmations. The purpose of affirmation for me is to replace a better thought than I had before. Meditation helps me slow my mind down. Prayers are my intentional re-coding of the mind.

What I put in my body plays a significant role in my energy, influencing my mood based on how I feel about myself. Am I getting enough movement and exercise? My husband always jokes, "You never see a depressed person with a six-pack." It is essential to incorporate some form of movement, but finding balance, resting, and relaxing overall is essential to respecting your body.

Your Spirit is perfect. Whatever spiritual practices you enjoy, immerse yourself in it.

Fun involves my free time, like hobbies, volunteer work, and community service. Giving of my time, shining my light in places I can give back. What you give, you get back. The feeling you feel when you help others is what you give, not so much on the physical thing, but the feeling behind the physical is what you give. So, if you are doing something physically, but, internally, you do not want to, that is the energy you are truly giving. It is necessary to do what makes you happy.

Finance. How can you earn money through a career, entrepreneurial, or investment path?

Money is how our economic system keeps the wheel turning. Late in life, I understood I needed to learn to earn, not make money. People make money daily by printing it. I needed to add more value to myself and others to earn more money. Value is not a price tag; it is your belief in yourself and the ability to demand more.

Ships. I had to learn to nurture all different relationships, including family, friends, and mentors. It is vital to build rich relationships with people who are doing what you want to do. They have firsthand experience and are better equipped with knowledge to help guide you. Sometimes, you also have to cut some relationships if they are not helping you grow and become your better self. Build a healthy relationship with your routines, strategies, and plans, and stay loyal to them.

The Redemption of My Soul

In Matthew 16:13 Jesus asks his disciples, "Who do people say that I am?" They answered him with the people's response. In today's world, I believe the answers would be according to your area of interest. If your circle is centered around religion, it may sound like some say you are broken, lost, a teacher, a sinner, a saint, a savior, a Baptist, a Church of God, etc. If your circle is centered around politics, they would say left-wing, right-wing, libertarian, etc. If your circle is centered around societal status, it may sound like you are a victim, you are oppressed, you are an outcast, you are rich, you are poor, etc. Whatever you are defending would be what they say you are.

Jesus heard what people thought of him. It is okay for others to form their own opinions of you; that is their free will to use their imagination. The most important thought you must attain is in the next question Jesus asked: *Who do you say I am? Peter answered, "You are the Messiah, son of the living God."* (Matthew 16:15)

In my journey from victimhood to resilience to self-empowerment and self-love, I am the one who must take my message higher. I am the daughter of the Living God. It is not what others think of me or what I want others to think of me; it is who I believe I am. If I believe I am a victim, then I am a victim. If I believe I am broken, then I am broken. If I believe I cannot, then I cannot. If I believe I can, then I can. If I believe I will not get the job because of the color of my skin, then I will not get the job because of my skin color. If I believe I am not loved, then I am not loved. If I believe I am not worthy, then I am not worthy. To be clear, even if someone believes I can and cannot, *I cannot until I believe I can.*

The world does not need to change for me to believe in myself. It is perfect. Within it are our beliefs and our pursuit of action and reactions. Jesus sealed Peter's answer with the statement upon this rock (what you believe), I will build my church (you are the church), and nothing shall prevail against your belief. It is done unto us as we believe.

On this rock, I redeemed my soul and let go of all the labels and the blame. I learned to stand *on* my story and not *in* it. I realized that if I deactivated all the perceived enemies that I had built up inside, I would be left with just myself. Self is stillness. Stillness is presence. Presence is love. Love is God.

To answer the title of this book, I must ask myself the following question: *Why did I hate myself?* The best answer I could come up with was because I did not understand who I was. Solomon, the man of great wisdom, said in Proverbs 4:7, *"In all thy getting, get understanding."* God is love. I am love. You are loved. We are love. We are one. A lecture or a story cannot uncover this journey, but through personal experience, that's what makes it real. If you experience it, it is no longer a question but the answer. X marks the spot no matter the direction. What I was looking for was myself. Myself was the problem and also the answer. Fear not; God is with you always. Be still and know thyself.

To be conscious is to take control of my mind. Some say wake up or level up, and all insinuate the same understanding. The mind serves me just like technology was designed to help us. I now use my mind to serve me, not vice versa. I became transformed by the renewal of my mind and not conforming to what I see in the world. What we see in the world is what we already created. What we do not see is what we are currently creating.

It all narrows down to the path of choice, choosing what I will consciously create in our amazing world. I am creating from love, love of God, and for all regardless of our external differences, and also from fear, fear of how powerful God is. True empowerment is in finding the balance to stay consistent and remain disciplined and teachable. I am the head, not the tail, above my experiences, and I am genuinely at peace with myself.

The peace of God took me off the cross of my mental and emotional suffering, and I declared the past was over. It is finished because I own it. Everything I need is inside of me. I am the full package; therefore, I was free to give myself the freedom to thrive. I allowed myself to feel my emotions, nurture my awareness, and watch my life manifest my inner conception.

My family and I embody the living word of love, compassion, health, wealth, and happiness. We are human beings, living fully present. I will end this chapter of my life with my famous quote: I love to give everywhere I go, and it is:

Life is a gift, and how we live our lives is the gift we give to ourselves and the world.

Suppose you do not know where to start your transition or you just need a shift on your journey. Maybe you are not ready yet or need some inspiration. Let me share with you what I started with; feel free to use it, but most importantly, get understanding.

The entire universe is working together for my good. Nothing is stopping me from growing and expanding. I love myself with all my heart and mind. I love everything about myself. I love how adaptable I am. I love how I navigate through life with ease. I love to encourage myself and lift my spirit. All things work together for my good. Everything or project I work on turns out great and with room for growth, and I am open to learning new things and exposing myself to new opportunities. I am very blessed, and I know that. The light of love shines ever so bright in and around me. I salute the divine light in everyone and give thanks for all my creativity and bravery.

I am the salt and light of my world and well-seasoned with kindness and compassion toward myself. I live a blissful and prosperous life and am thankful to be alive and well. Everything I touch turns to gold and is very productive. I listen to my spirit, which always steers me in the right direction. I never fail; I grow. I am exactly where I need to be doing what I am doing. My life aligns perfectly, and I find balance in everything.

I am thankful for a higher level of awareness. I am living a better life daily. I love everything about my life. I am satisfied and content. I am filled with peace and a greater understanding of myself. I live an abundant life with more than enough. I refuel when I give; therefore, I love to give; giving contributes to my happiness. The more I give, the more I receive. This is my season of receiving, and I receive well. I eat well. I sleep well. I speak well. I write well. I create well. I take care of myself well. I perceive well. I care for my family well. I love you well. I create wealth well. I live well.

ABOUT THE AUTHOR

Stephanie Harrington is the CEO of Create Her, a company dedicated to empowering women to achieve their personal and professional goals. With a background in Life Coaching, Stephanie uses her knowledge and experiences to help her clients activate their willpower and reclaim their lives.

As a published author and speaker, Stephanie is committed to sharing her message of personal growth and self-love with women everywhere. Her ultimate goal is to help women live their highest expression of themselves, whether that means financial freedom, or simply living a life filled with love and fulfillment.

www.ingramcontent.com/pod-product-compliance
Lightning Source LLC
Chambersburg PA
CBHW020244130626
46549CB00005B/2054